Girls, Girls, Girls

By
Ferrell K. Hill

(Mrs. A. R. Hill, Sr.)

Published by

J. C. Choate Publications
Burton Drive
Winona, Mississippi 38967
U.S.A.

First Printing, 1980
Typesetting, Sam Boyd Enterprise, Singapore
Offset Printing, U.S.A.
Art Work, Tim Hacker and Steve Choate
Proof Reading, Gordon Hogan

Dedication

Dedicated to: Jolly Hill Pryor, our beloved daughter. "Many daughters have done worthily, but thou excelleth them all." (Proverbs 31:29)

Foreword

When the publication of *The World Evangelist* was begun in August 1972, I was asked to write a column entitled UNTO YOU, YOUNG WOMEN. Basil Overton, the Editor, thought a mature woman should be the writer, according to Titus 2:3–5. It is not the mother, or sister that the young girl wants to go to for soul talks. Why? Because grandmothers know how to bridge that "generation gap" with love and understanding. "Be age the guide of youth; both will be happy only if they go hand in hand together." — *Goethe.*

An old Dutch proverb says: "Good leading makes good following." Grandmothers have always seemed to get along well with the young ones because thy know what youngsters like. That is why their cookie jars are always full of goodies and why their refrigerators contain plenty of cold milk and lemonade.

I think grandmothers remember what it was like to be small and active with an inquiring mind. Golda Meier said: "It is no sin to be seventy!" Grandmother knows that it is no sin to be *seven* or *seventeen* and she is very sympathetic. Therefore she has a listening ear. She also is a good story teller, using homespun parables, to teach principles of righteousness. Her counsel is given in the light of God's word.

This little book is a compilation of columns chosen from "UNTO YOU, YOUNG WOMEN" in *The World Evangelist*. It is our prayer that the young readers will be encouraged to become better persons.

Ferrell K. Hill
(Mrs. A. R. Hill, Sr.)

Introduction

As a Christian mother and grandmother, and at a time when most women would be thinking of slowing up and resting on past accomplishments, Sis. Ferrell K. Hill (Mrs. A. R. Hill, Sr.) continues to go forward. Over the years she has excelled as a preacher's wife, Bible teacher, and writer. She is a promoter of the Christian home and Christian education. She is a painter, puppet maker, and a doer of good works.

Sis. Hill has worked along side her husband, a faithful Gospel preacher, in a number of States, after meeting, courting, and marrying at David Lipscomb College in Nashville, Tenn. While being a preacher's wife, caring for their home, helping to rear their children, she also had time to write for several years a series of the Gospel Advocate Quarterly. Later she wrote a popular children's book, Home on Dogwood Hill, and more recently, UNTO YOU YOUNG WOMEN , KEEPERS OF THE HOME, to be used to help raise funds in the interest of International Bible College at Florence, Alabama. And finally, this book is being printed and who knows how many more may follow.

The Hills make their home now at 315 Wright Drive, Florence, Alabama. Bro. and Sis. Hill continue to be active in preaching and teaching God's word. My wife and I have come to know them more personally only during the past few years, but we have learned to love and appreciate them. We have been in their home on several occasions and it is always a real delight to be around them.

It is with a great deal of pleasure for me to be able to print some of Sis. Hill's books here in the States and it is my prayer that the Lord will continue to bless the Hill's and their every effort to further the cause of Christ.

Within the pages of this book you will find many articles of good Christian reading. Being directed to women of all ages, but especially to young women, you are encouraged to help us to place this book in the hands of as many people as possible. It needs to be in each Christian home, in every church library, in Bible classes, and anywhere else where people can be influenced to live for the Lord.

With these words we then submit to you this book which has been written by a fine Christian woman, directed to women, and through whom this material can be used again and again to bless them, to exalt their maker, and to make the world a better place in which to live.

J. C. Choate
Church of Christ
131 Moulmein Road
Singapore 1130
February 1, 1980

Suggestion To The Teachers

Teachers of teen age girls will find material in all areas of Christian living in the form of inspirational articles on the following subjects: Controling the Tongue, Selecting a Life Companion, Caring For Pets, Modest Dress, Conservation and Patriotism, Prayer, The Thrill of a Driver's License at Age Sixteen, Handling Temptation, Choosing Friends.

Since youth is the seed time of life, girls need encouragement and challenge in making choices. Young people do not learn just because adults wish them to learn. Our aim is to plant principles of righteousness and truth, from the word of the Lord, in the hearts of our readers. Our job is to create a desire to learn and grow to maturity as responsible Christians.

The lessons in this book will fit in with projects planned by the teachers. The girls might enjoy making some posters or bulletin boards to illustrate some of the lessons. "Whom Shall We Invite To Dinner" might inspire a benevolent project of visiting nursing homes or children's hospitals. A study of "Heart Portraits" could cause the girls to want to honor their mothers with a tea or luncheon. From the Chinese we have this proverb: "Tell me, I'll forget; show me, I may remember; but involve me and I'll understand."

Ferrel K. Hill
(Mrs. A.R. Hill, Sr.)

Contents

CHAPTER I

God Ordained Teachers

All babies are sweet, but girl babies are more angelic. Little boys are cute, but little girls are especially adorable. Girls do go through an awkward age, but then they blossom into womanhood. What is more lovely than a young girl "growing in grace and knowledge" adding the Christian virtues? She is like a rose bud, unfolding into the full grown rose, beauty coming from within.

At some stage of her development, every woman needs a guide, teacher, counselor and friend, outside the home. God in his wisdom has supplied this need. The apostle Paul, writing to the young preacher, Titus, about sound doctrine, gives instruction about aged women. (Titus 2:3, 4.) Mature women in the church, who have developed to a high degree in the Christian life are God ordained teachers. Not to the young preacher did the Holy Spirit through Paul entrust this responsibility of teaching young women, but to those better qualified, older women, who have been tempered by time, wisdom and experience. "Old enough to know and young enough to care," as Mark Harris said about Carl Sandburg (84) and Robert Frost (87) in Life Magazine.

It has been suggested that Titus 2:3—5 applies only to mothers teaching in the home. If this passage were addressed to individual mothers, why was the word daughters not used instead of young women? We must also remember that Paul is speaking to aged women, whose daughters were already married with homes of their own.

If we think of Titus 2:3—5 applying to all aged women in the congregation qualified as teachers, there is no infringement on the duties and responsibilities of parents. Ephesians 4:4 is addressed to fathers. Both boys and girls in every Christian

1

home are so trained. We have the example of Timothy, who from a babe was taught the sacred writings by a godly mother and grandmother. (1 Timothy 1:5; 2 Timothy 3:14.)

It is sad, but true, that many young women in the church were not reared in Christian homes. Others have not had opportunities to learn how Christian girls should act when they go out on dates; what kind of husband to choose for a life companion; what is the meaning of chastity; how to be a real help-mate for a Christian husband; how to be a home maker, wife and mother, pleasing to God in all things; the advantages of being "workers (keepers) at home" instead of taking jobs in shops and factories.

Paul clearly describes the teacher and her work. (Titus 2:3—5.) "That aged women likewise be reverent in demeanor, not slanderers nor enslaved to much wine, teachers of that which is good." Notice there are two positive and two negative characteristics mentioned. How different were women in the early church from Christian women today? We know that manners and customs change, but principles of righteousness and human nature are the same in every century.

Let us consider the meaning of "reverent in demeanor" (in behavior as becometh holiness.) Perhaps worshippers of the true God were to be in contrast to the pagans. Today, Christian women differ from worldly minded people in dress and conduct. In our grandmothers we admire godliness, poise and dignity. Giddy and frivolous are not fitting words to describe them, because they act their age, but rather gracious and dignified are better words.

To the mature women there is a warning: "Be not slanderers nor enslaved to much wine." It has been said that woman's greatest fault is talking too much. Older women, who no longer have the responsibilities of a growing family, perhaps have more leisure time and fall into the bad habit of gossiping. Slander is the crime of injuring a person's good name by spreading false reports about him. Surely, no Christian woman would be guilty of this crime! It is all right to talk, if like the worthy woman of old, "She openeth her mouth with wisdom and the law of kindness is on her tongue." (Proverbs 31:26.) It is good to be friendly and sociable, but social drinking may lead to alcoholism, which would surely cause one to become a slave to the habit. A generation or two ago it was not uncommon for "granny" to smoke her pipe by the fireside and take a little nip of brandy or home brew. However, her modern counterpart, in this atomic age has made progress. Mature women in the church do not drink intoxicating beverages today, but live busy, useful lives, as "teachers of that which is good."

It is impossible to think of a saintly grandmother at a discotheque, engaging in disgusting gyrations of the body, dressed in hot pants, smoking tobacco or "pot" or "grass," gossiping as she drinks cocktails! Mature women in the church today are shining examples of Christian motherhood, who teach by precept and example. When their talents are so used, juvenile delinquency and divorce problems will decrease. When we listen, learn and follow the divine admonitions, this will be a better and happier world.

The job assigned to the aged women, by Paul through the Holy Spirit is, "that they may train the young women to love their husbands, to love their children, to be sober-minded, chaste, workers at home, kind, being in subjection to their own husbands, that the word of God be not blasphemed." (Titus 2:4, 5) When this plan, set forth by Paul, for training young women is not followed the word of God is blasphemed. It is a serious matter to neglect so important a work.

When the world sees so-called Christian homes broken

by divorce (caused by philandering husbands, unfaithful wives, selfishness, laziness, in-laws, money matters or what) they speak disrespectfully of the church. When undisciplined children coming from such homes, get in trouble at school or with the law, parents and church members are blamed and rightly so.

According to an old proverb, "Prevention is better than cure." How many congregations of Christ have regular training classes for young women concerning the marriage relationship, modest dress, chastity, the new morality, situation ethics, taught by a God ordained teacher? Is this teaching needed in our brotherhood? Thousands of sober-minded Christians say "yes." Let us not criticize the youngsters for wrong doing, when we as mature Christians have failed to teach them God's word. This column is designed to fill a need and we pray that God will bless our efforts.

"If" For Girls

If you can fill life full of wholesome pleasure
    Yet not make fun your only end and aim;
If you can row and swim, play golf and tennis,
    And yet keep sweet and girlish just the same;
If you can lead your class in school or college
    And yet not feel that you have learned it all;
Or, being slow, see others pass you,
    Rejoice with them, yet not feel that you're small;
If you can like the boys and win their favor,
    Yet not one minute lose your self-respect;
But make each one you talk with feel the stronger
    And glad to live the life that you expect;
If you can dress in style and be attractive
    Yet do not think that clothes count more than brains;

4

If you can mix with those of wealth and culture,
    Yet see that simple courtesy remains;
If you can meet with heartaches and keep cheery,
    Have discouragements, yet rise above them all;
If you can make the world the better,
    Bring cheer to lonely hearts and help to all;
If you can win the love of little children
        And help to keep their lives sweet, pure and true
        You'll grow to splendid woman hood, my dear one,
        And be of service, whatso'er you do.

— Ina Hogg

Fulfilment

The maiden prayed: "God make me beautiful,
Endow me with such fairness that the world
Shall see and own me fair, Oh, grant me power
Great as Egypt's queen, that men, all men,
Shall call me beautiful beyond compare."

The woman prayed: "God give me power of song;
A voice to thrill and hold the hearts of men.
And make them subjects — slaves of each caprice;
For fires that rage within — I'd find a vent
In song — Oh, grant me, God, the power of song."

And God seemed not to hear; but gave her Life
To live. To maid and woman, sorrows fell
That filled each day and night with pain until
Of all was left her but a woman's soul,
That yet had learned its lesson well; then came
A beauty in her face unknown, undreamed;
So great her power she feared its wrong appliance,
And prayed each day for light and strength,

5

And music stole into her voice — deep notes
That thrilled men's lives and stirred weak souls to act;
And her power was great beyond compare.
Thus God, inscrutable, doth answer prayer.

— Anonymous

God answers sharp and sudden prayers,
And thrusts the thing we have prayed for in our face,
A gauntlet with a gift in't. Every wish
Is like a prayer, with God.

— Elizabeth Barrett Browning

Some hearts, like evening primroses open more beautifully in the shadows of life.

Menu For the Mind

I want this day to be a cheerful and successful one, so that I may come to my resting bed tonight glad and satisfied. To accomplish this I will plan my day intelligently. Since I know that happiness depends on my will and attitude of mind and not on events, I will adjust myself to what happens. Therefore I am resolved that:

    1. I will not worry. If a thing can be helped, I will help it; if not, I will make the best of it.

    2. I will keep all mental poisons out of my thoughts.

3. I will especially resist and exclude fear which weakens and unnerves me.

4. I will not allow myself to become angry.

5. I will resist pride.

6. I will try to affect pleasantly every one with whom I am thrown in contact.

7. I will try to make happiness as well as receive it.

8. I will believe in myself. I will allow nothing to make me doubt myself nor create in me discouragement or despair.

9. I will not let myself despise any human being, and I will keep all contemptuous and condemnatory thoughts of anybody out of my mind.

10. I will keep my whole self in tune with positive and healthful optimistic forces.

11. I will get along without friction or bickering, or strained relations, with my family, my neighbors and business associates.

12. I will plan for at least a half hour's quiet, for prayer, for reflection, and for cultivation of my own spirit.

13. I will be more honest, square and prompt than business demands; more thoughtful than love requires.

14. I will do somebody a good turn, that is not expected of me.

15. If any person does me wrong, I will not bear him a grudge, I will try to forget it.

16. I will enjoy as heartily as I can what the day brings me, and also try to get pleasure from the simple and common things; eating, drinking, resting, so that at night I may be able to say that I have lived and found life good today.

– Author unknown

I found the "Menu For the Mind" in an old scrap book. Perhaps it will help us to start off the New Year. I suggest that we read Phillipians 4:8, 9. " . . . that the God of peace shall be with you."

LIFE IS A STORY

Life is a story, in volumes three:
The Past, the Present, and YET TO BE;
The first we have finished and laid away'
The second we are reading day by day;
The third and the last of these volumes three
Is locked from sight — God keepeth the key.

LOOK

Look back and give thanks;
    Look forward and take courage.
        Don't pin your faith — nail it!

Topics For Discussion:

1. Two positive and two negative characteristics of God ordained teachers for young women. (Titus 2:3.)
2. Training for marriage. (Titus 2:4, 5.)
3. How the word is blasphemed when this training is neglected.
4. Mothers train their children in the home; aged women train young women in the church for marriage — no conflict.
5. Each if in "If For Girls."
6. The maiden's prayer; the woman's prayer; God's answer in Fulfilment.

7. Change the Menu of The Mind to make it fit your own resolutions.
8. How Life can be divided into three volumes.
9. Whether or not you agree with "Look."
10. Why fasten securely your faith.

CHAPTER II

Eagles Don't Fly In Flocks

"Aw, everybody else is doing it." Have you ever given that as a reason to do something that your parents did not think you should do? Perhaps you did not really believe that it was the right thing to do, but only wanted to be with the crowd.

Most of us find it hard to be different. It is easy to swim with the current and hard to swim against it. It is easy to follow but more difficult to be a leader, or to resist when you know the crowd is in the wrong.

It will help you at times like that to remember the eagle. He is a great, majestic bird. He suggests strength and nobility just by his appearance. Eagles do not follow the crowd. They do not fly in flocks. The eagle will go his own way, the one his instinct tells him is right, regardless of what others are doing. So when in doubt about what others are doing, and wondering if you should follow them, remember th eagle. When it would be more pleasant to follow the lead of others, but you feel that it is wrong, be an eagle.

Worms For Sale

It is an old fable, but it still is worth repeating. A lark, singing in the high branches of a tree, saw a traveler walking through the forest carrying a mysterious little black box. The lark flew down and perched on the man's shoulder.

"What do you have in the little black box?" the lark asked. "Worms", the traveler replied. "Are they for sale?" questioned the bird. "Yes, and very cheap, too, the price is only one feather" was the answer.

The lark thought for a moment. "I must have a million feathers, most of them quite small. Surely I will never miss one of them. Here is an opportunity to get a good dinner for no work at all." He told the man that he would buy one.

He searched carefully under his wing for a tiny, tiny feather. He winced a bit as he pulled it out, but the size and quality of the worm make him quickly forget the pain. High up in the tree he began to sing as beautifully as before.

The next day he saw the same man and once more he exchanged a feather for a worm. What a wonderful way to get dinner — and no effort at all!

We skip the next day, and the next, for we are sure you are ahead of the story. In any event, he lost a feather each day and each loss seemed to hurt less and less. Finally, after the loss of one of his primary feathers, he could no longer reach the top of the tree or soar into the sky. The lark no longer sang, because he was ashamed of his fallen state.

This is how unworthy habits possess us. First painfully, then more easily until at last we find ourselves stripped of all that lets us soar and sing. This is how our freedom in Christ is lost; sacrificing one by one Christian virtues for pleasures.

You Tell On Yourself

You tell on yourself by the friends you seek,
By the manner in which you speak,
By the way you employ your leisure time,
By the use you make of dollar and dime.
You tell what you are by the things you wear,
By the spirit in which you burdens bear,

By the kind of things at which you laugh,
By records you play on the record player.
You tell what you are by the way you walk,
By the things of which you delight to talk,
By the manner in which you bear defeat,
By so simple a thing as how you eat,
By the books you choose for the well filled shelf.
So there's really no particle of sense,
In any effort at false pretense.

Topics For Discussion:

1. Why the eagle was chosen as our national bird.
2. Wisdom of following a leader without thinking for oneself.
3. Why the lark could no longer soar in the sky.
4. Examples of Christian virtues sacrificed for pleasure.
5. "She that giveth herself to pleasure is dead while she liveth." (I Timothy 5:6.) Distinguish between kinds of pleasure.
6. Compare above passage to Luke 15:24 (story of prodigal son.)
7. A dozen way to "Tell on Yourself."

CHAPTER III

Who Is On Trial?

Tourists were visiting a famous picture gallery as part of a sightseeing tour. They went around the gallery in a gallop, taking only a few minutes to view the works of art. Having completed the circuit, they manifested a total lack of appreciation for the value and beauty of the paintings by these remarks to the custodian: "We don't think much of this collection!" The official replied: "It does not matter what you think, these pictures are not on trial!"

Isn't it strange how we pass judgment on ourselves? The fault was not with the masterpieces in the gallery, but rather with those who were viewing them. Often non-thinking or immoral people will say: "The Bible is out of date, quite old-fashioned; the new morality or situation ethics is 'in'; we decide for ourselves what is right or wrong according to the circumstances; we do not need a musty old book to tell us what to do!"

How wrong, ignorant or just plain stupid can people be in thinking that they do not need the Bible today? The Bible is the word of God, who is the great Creator of the universe. We recognize our God as the all-wise, all-powerful and self-sufficient one. "No word from God shall be void of power." (Luke 1:37.) This book is not for any special time or place or people, but for all ages and races, around the world. God is from everlasting to everlasting (Psalm 90:2.) and so is his word. Without the Bible, the whole human race is like a ship at sea without chart or compass. David realized that we need a light on our path as we walk through the darkness of sin and ignorance in this jungle of life. (Psalm 119:105.) On the way to heaven, the Bible is our road map. If we follow this infallible guide book, we can feel secure. Without it, we are lost in the world of Satanic rule. The prophet

13

recognized this truth centuries ago. "It is not in man that walketh to direct his steps." (Jeremiah 10:23.)

Customs may, and do change, but principles of truth and righteousness never change. They are as eternal and as unchangeable as God himself, and can not be changed to suit the changing conditions of worldy wise people. The word Bible is derived from a Greek word meaning a book. Since it contains God's will to man, it is the Book of books. It is the best, most valuable, and in many respects the most popular book in the world. Millions of copies of this best seller are printed every year in many languages. This book is the most valuable in the world, because we will be saved by the gospel (good news) message in it. (Romans 1:16.) We will also be judged by it at the end of the world. (Romans 2:16.) We can not get along without the Bible for it is the rule book for the game of life. All sports and games have rule books and the Bible shows us how to live, work and play in every relationship of this life: parents and children; husbands and wives, employee and employer; neighbors and friends; government officials and citizens; servants in the church.

The Bible is a library of sixty-six books, all genuine masterpieces. It has withstood all critics down through the centuries. It is not the Bible on trial in our time, my friend, but you! Do you read it, love it and live by it?

Prayer Reminders

Man's greatest avenue of power is prayer. Any child of God has access to it continually. There is no "red tape" to go through in order to reach God; no waiting in line in order to speak to the Great Creator. One never gets a "busy signal" when one wishes to communicate with God, although there may be millions of others doing the same thing.

It almost staggers the imagination to consider what a marvelous privilege to have a "hot line" directly to heaven, day or night! Do we really understand and appreciate this divine gift within our reach? How may we utilize the power at our finger tips? Why question its reality?

"If radio's slim fingers can pluck a melody
From night and toss it over a continent or sea;
If the petalled white notes of a violin
Are blown across the mountains or the city's din;
If songs, like crimson roses, are culled from thin blue air
Why should mortals wonder if God hears prayer?"

— Edith Fuller

"Lord teach us to pray . . . " (Luke 11:1.)
WHEN? Without ceasing. (1 Thessalonians 5:17; Acts 2:42.)
WHERE? Everywhere. (1 Timothy 2:8.)
WHO? The righteous. (James 5:16.)

CONDITIONS OF ACCEPTABLE PRAYER

1. In faith. (James 1:5, Hebrews 11:6.)
2. In the name of Christ. (John 14:14.)
3. According to his will. (1 John 5:14.)
4. In spirit of forgiveness. (Matthew 6:12–14.)

WASTED PRAYERS

1. Iniquity in the heart. (Psalm 66:18.)
2. Refusal to hear the law. (Proverbs 28:9.)
3. Hypocrisy — for show, to seem pious. (Matthew 6:5.)
4. Vain repetitions. (Matthew 6:7.)

5. Asking amiss — selfish. (James 4:3.)
6. Boastful. (Luke 18:9—14.)

HOW? THE MODEL PRAYER (MATTHEW 6:9—13.)

Divine model in brevity, simplicity and comprehension. It embraces: (1) The honor of God; (2) Extension of his kingdom; (3) The salvation of the human race; (4) Our spiritual and temporal needs. In these petitions: (1) Hallowed be thy name; (2) Thy will be done; (3) Give us this day our daily bread; (4) Forgiveness; (5) Bring us not into temptation; (6) Deliver us from evil.

PERSEVERANCE IN PRAYER

1. Selfish man. (Luke 11:5—8.) Ask, seek and knock.
2. The widow and the judge. (Luke 18:1—8.) "Ought always to pray and not to faint."

LESSON IN HUMILITY AND SELF RIGHTEOUSNESS

Pharisee and Publican. (Luke 18:9—14.)

PRAYER REMINDERS

MORNING.
1. Talk to God. Put your day in his hands.

2. Ask him to help you act as a real Christian in all of your activities, both work and play.

3. Give thanks for your blessings Name them.

4. Ask his blessings on others.

ALL DAY.

1. Select some symbol as a reminder of God's presence. For instance: your watch or a clock — each minute belongs to God.

2. If you use a typewriter, any factory machine, or at home a sewing machine or vacuum-cleaner — think, "I am an instrument in God's hand."

3. Each day as you use an elevator, escalator or steps . . . think . . . "I want to climb higher toward my God and Christian ideals."

4. Let the transportation you use (automobile, trolley, bus or train) remind you that Christians are only sojourners, tourists, travelling through this world temporarily, our home is heaven.

NIGHT.

1. Give an account to God, who has entrusted you with a day. Go over the events of the day as a faithful steward.

2. Ask forgiveness for the mistakes of the day.

3. Let praise,. thanksgiving and intercessions for others ascend to the throne of God.

4. Put away from your mind the business and cares of the day.

5. Rest in God's care.

PRAYING HANDS

First reach above
    To catch the hands of one
Who times the planets
    Paints the crystal dawn.

Then reach below
 To share the human load
For hands in prayer
 Become the hands of God.

— *Olive McGuire*

Topics for discussion:

1. Your evaluation of the Bible.
2. Message in Romans 1:16.
3. Difference in customs and principles.
4. Man's greatest avenue of power.
5. A "hot line" to heaven.
6. Conditions of acceptable prayer.
7. Wasted prayers — why?
8. The model prayer.
9. Our lesson from the widow and the judge.
10. Difference in the Pharisee and Publican (Luke 18:9–14.)
11. Your prayer reminders.
12. Christians as tourists in this world.
13. How the hands in prayer become the hands of God.

CHAPTER IV

A Valentine

Oh little loveliest lady mine,
　　What shall I send for your valentine?
Summer and flowers are far away;
　　Gloomy old Winter is king today.
Buds will not glow, and sun will not shine;
　　What shall I do for a valentine?

Prithee, St. Valentine, tell us more,
　　Why do you come at this time of year?
Plenty of days when lilies are white,
　　Plenty of days when sunbeams are bright.
But now, when eveything's dark and drear,
　　Why do you come, St. Valentine dear?

I've searched the gardens all through and through,
　　For a bud to tell of my love so true.
But buds were asleep and blossoms were dead,
　　And the falling snow came down on my head.
So, little loveliest lady mine,
　　Here is MY HEART FOR YOUR VALENTINE!

— Laura E. Richards

About this time of the year I have to make decisions about what to throw away and what to keep when spring cleaning comes. Have you heard this definition of a desk? "A waste basket with drawers in it." That description fits mine. How about this definition of a filing cabinet? "A place where one loses things alphabetically." At my house, there is a tendency to let useless junk pile up.

In our spiritual lives, it is good to have a spring cleaning. We could discard worry, nagging words, bad tempers and selfishness, which are useless bits of junk.

We must be sure to "KEEP THY HEART WITH ALL DILIGENCE FOR OUT OF IT ARE THE ISSUES OF LIFE." (Proverbs 4:23.) Keep means to guard or defend, protect or observe. There are many ways of keeping things: by care, strength, or by calling in help. Lincoln said "Keep thy heart from discouragement."

In President Carter's inaugural address, I was impressed with the words: "In these changing times, we must hold to unchanging principles." He also quoted Micah 6:8" "What doth the Lord require of thee but to do justly, and to show mercy and to walk humbly with thy God?" It was Solomon who said: "As a man thinketh within himself so is he "Proverbs 23:7.)

The Cupboards Of The Heart

I have just been cleaning cupboards and with house-wifely art,
    I have set things all in order in the storehouse of my heart.
There are things I always meant to save and look at every day.
    And then again, a lot of things I should have thrown away.

There are things in wild disorder, and mixed among the lot,
    Were bitter things, and ugly ones that should have been forgot.
But there are scraps of tender dreams — a child's remembered kiss,
    A poem my mother wrote — ah how I treasured this.

I discovered that, that ugly things were taking too much space.
    Sometimes for new and lovely ones, I couldn't find a place!
And so I've tossed the dark things out — the sullen scraps and tatters,
    Of old-time hurts and fancied wrongs and here's what really matters.

Now that I've tossed the dark things out — each cringing one I found,
   The others shine the brighter and shed radiance all around!
My cleaning work is nearly done, and I suggest you start,
   For you'll find it's mighty nice to have clean cupboards IN YOUR
HEART!

– Author Unknown

A Red Letter Day

Attention! All readers approaching your sixteenth birthday.
This date is important, because one can apply for a driver's
license! Of course this is altogether different from a learner's
permit. What gives a sixteen year old more prestige than a
license to drive a car? It makes one feel very superior and
grown-up. However, with the ability to handle a powerful
machine, plus the opportunity, comes the responsibility.

Many centuries ago, before the automobile age, people
were guilty of reckless driving. Horse driven chariots were
common methods of transportation. Jehu, the tenth king of
Israel, was a driver we do not care to imitate. The following
is copied from the International Bible Encyclopaedia. "Jehu
was bold, daring, unscrupulous, and masterful and astute in
his policy, BUT ONE SEEKS IN VAIN IN HIS CHARAC-
TER FOR ANY TOUCH OF MAGNANIMITY OF THE
FINER QUALITIES OF THE RULER. His zeal for Jehovah
was too largely a cloak for merely worldly ambition. The
blood shed in which his rule was founded early provoked
a reaction and his closing years were dark with trouble."

The watchman standing on the tower in Jezreel saw a
company of men approaching the city. He said: "The
driving is like the driving of Jehu, the son of Nimshi; FOR
HE DRIVETH FURIOUSLY." (2 Kings 9:20.) Even afar off

Jehu was recognized because of his driving.

Let us resolve, as newly licensed drivers, to take our privilege seriously and be recognized as driving safely and courteously. Teenagers can make a very fine contribution to our country in this respect. It is one way of showing our patriotism.

Much fruitful work has been done in the last twenty years by legislators, law enforcement agencies, traffic court judges, motor vehicle administrators, educators, highway and traffic engineers, as well as traffic safety organizations throughout the country to stem the frightening tide of motor vehicle accidents.

But it is apparent that all this is not enough. Despite governmental and civic efforts, traffic accidents have caused thousands of fatalities and millions of injuries annually over the past years.

A new ingredient, a new approach to the problem is needed. Traffic safety leaders are hopeful that a sense of MORAL RESPONSIBILITY at the wheel may prove to be the ingredient needed to slash the horrendous traffic toll. Teenagers can be leaders to the rest of the nation. They are bright, alert, ambitious and anxious to do great things in the world. This is a good place to start. Teenagers can do anything they make up their minds to do. What can older people do to supply the motivation?

We all know that it is selfish acts of motorists that bring tragedy daily to countless homes. We should observe THE GOLDEN RULE on the highway by driving lawfully, carefully and courteously. Maintaining cheerful, respectful attitude toward fellow motorists and pedestrians is also helpful. LOVE THY NEIGHBOR may be paraphrased LOVE THY FELLOW DRIVER!

Billy Graham is quoted as saying: "The Bible says, 'Thou shalt not kill.' A man is just as dead when murdered by an automobile as he is when killed with a gun, a knife, or poison. PRACTICE YOUR RELIGION IN TRAFFIC AS WELL AS IN CHURCH. When you, fellow Christian, start off on a trip, remind yourself that you are your brother's keeper and pray that by the grace of God, he may be yours."

THE MOTORIST'S PRAYER

"O God, give me a firm hand and a sharp eye so that I will not injure any person while driving. Thou hast given life and I pray that none of my actions will take away or spoil the gift which comes from thee. Grant that I may refrain from the kind of indulgence that would impair my skill and thus endanger the life and safety of my fellow man. Guide my automobile for the protection of others. And may I not miss, because of the love of speed, the beauty of the world which thou hast created. May I always drive courteously, safely and with a full sense of responsibility which lies in my hands. Amen."

Topics For Discussion:

1. The best valentine for one you love.
2. Discards at a spiritual spring cleaning time.
3. The Bible heart and the human mind are the same.
4. Ten adjectives describing the Bible heart.
5. Ability plus opportunity equals responsibility.
6. The life of Jehu.
7. One characteristic of Jehu that we do not want to imitate.
8. Showing patriotism in our driving.
9. Obeying The Golden Rule on the highways.
10. The Motorist's Prayer.

CHAPTER V

Honey

Girls, as we celebrate the birthday of Abraham Lincoln, this month I have a story for you from his childhood.

Lincoln was one of our truly great presidents. Many books have been written about his life and work, stressing his mercy and kindness. He is especially remembered for THE EMANCIPATION PROCLAMATION, or for freeing the slaves. However, the great heart of Lincoln was full of concern for all of God's creatures, both human and animal. This story from his boyhood days about his little dog, Honey, is an example.

The Lincoln family was moving from Kentucky to Indiana. It was in the winter and since the river was frozen over, it seemed a good time to make the crossing. All of their household goods was loaded on a wagon, pulled by oxen. The heavy wagon broke through the ice and was almost lost. After calling for help from the neighbors, the men managed to get the oxen and wagon safely to the other shore.

Abraham was so excited and upset about the near tragedy that he forgot about his pet until he heard a frantic barking. Honey, the dog had been left behind on the other side of the river. Mr. Lincoln was not inclined to bother with a dog. The boy pleaded, "Pa., please, please let me go get him!"

The family patiently waited while Abraham went back across the icy river for his beloved pet, which he could not bear to leave. Since a dog is a boy's best friend, cold and danger could not stop this boy from attempting a rescue of his friend. No doubt the boy was recalling the many happy hours he and his dog had spent in hunting. Perhaps the name he gave his pet was an endearing term as well as the color of his coat, golden like honey.

All pet lovers can understand Abraham's anxiety about his dog. Perhaps many of you have pets, from parakeets to ponies, that you care for deeply.

"A righteous man regardeth the life of his beast." (Proverbs 12:10.) It is true that all animal lovers do have a special regard for their animals. The word regard means: (1) to look at carefully; (2) to esteem; respect; (3) to consider; evaluate. All pet owners should do the same. It is wrong to neglect by failing to feed and water them regularly. It is cruel to mistreat or beat a smaller, weaker creature. If we are not willing to give some time and attention to our pets, then we should not have any for which we are responsible.

A Proverb A Day Will Keep The Tempter Away

"We cannot tell what may happen to us in the strange medley of life. But we can decide what happens in us, how we take it, what we do with — and that is what really counts in the end. How to take the raw stuff of life and make it a thing of worth and beauty — that is the test of living." — *Joesph Fort Newton.*

Is it easy for you to make up your mind? Do you have a hard time deciding what is best to do about certain matters? Perhaps we all have this problem at one time or another, but nevertheless decisions have to be made. The following definition is given to help us understand the meaning of decision:

(1) a judgment arrived at after deliberation; resolution of doubt or uncertainty. (2) unwavering firmness; prompt and definite determination.

Anybody can say, "I couldn't help it — I didn't know what to do! Now I am in trouble, help me!" Young women, God has given you intelligence to learn right from wrong and you are to make up your own mind about your actions. As Christians, you have all freedom, within the range of God's word. Learning how to make decisions is part of your spiritual training. Ability plus opportunity equals responsibility. Self control is one of the Christian graces which we are taught to add to our faith. (2 Peter 1:6—9.)

Let us apply the wisdom of Solomon to our lives by using this proverb: "As a ring of gold in a swine's snout, so is a fair woman without discretion." (Proverbs 11:22.) Discretion is a good word. Let's put it in our vocabulary. It means using good judgment in avoiding evil; prudence, caution.

Did you ever see a hog out on a farm with a ring in its nose? By chance, did you notice what material was used for a ring? For sure, it was not gold, silver or platinum, but just a wire ring. The farmer could not afford to buy gold rings to keep the hogs from rooting up the grass in his pasture. It would be just as much out of order to see a fair (beautiful) woman without discretion as to see a ring of gold in a filthy pig's snout. Think about that.

In using discretion, a lovely, attractive girl never puts herself in a compromising position. She keeps herself above reproach, so the enemies of God's people have no just cause to gossip about her. (1) She always dates boys with good reputations, not any riff-raff or strangers. She will never start dating a man not good enough to marry. (2) She never habitually accepts a ride home from the office or school, or an invitation out to eat, with a married man. (3) She never invites her boy friend to her house for a visit, when her parents are not at home, either day or night. (4) She never stays out on a date into the wee hours of the morning, but returns home at the time her parents expect her. In case of a delay, she telephones home.

Even though we know what we ought to do, every Christian will be tempted. "Wherefore let him that thinketh he standeth take heed lest he fall. There hath no temptation taken you but such as man can bear: but God is faithful, who will not suffer you to be tempted above that ye are able; but will with the temptation make also the way of escape, that ye may be able to endure it." (2 Corinthians 10:12, 13.)

There is nothing sinful in temptation itself, but yielding to temptation is sinful. James tells us in the first chapter, verses two and three: "Count it all joy my brethren, when ye fall into manifold temptations; knowing that the proving of your faith worketh patience."

We learn that temptation is a testing and proving of our strength. In the same chapter, verses 23—24 James continues, "Blessed is the man that endureth temptation; for when he hath been approved, he shall receive the crown of life which the Lord promised to them that love him. Let no man say when he is tempted, I am tempted of God; for God cannot be tempted with evil, and he himself tempteth no man: but each man is tempted, when he is drawn away by his own lust an enticed."

There are different ways to deal with temptation. Paul gave the Ephesians instructions how to stand and fight. (Ephesians 6:10—17.) He also told Timothy to "Flee youthful lusts, and follow after righteousness, faith, love, peace, with them that call on the Lord out of a pure heart." (2 Timothy 2:22.) Does this apply to young people in the 20th Century as well as to Timothy?

Flee means to run, escape, take shelter from. Youthful suggests that there are possibly desires, drives and longings which are more characteristic of adolesence and do not belong either to childhood or adulthood, namely: over zealous, rash, proud, conceited, rebellious, stubborn, sullen, willfull, uncontrolled temper and tongue, over ambitious — often leading to dishonesty, both cheating and stealing, also passions for sexual indulgence easily aroused. Paul's advice still holds good.

It is not cowardly to run from danger, but shows good sense. If a group of hikers saw a rattle snake on the trail, they would surely run from him. If a mad dog appears in a neighborhood, all the people get out of his way and call the police. We are all taught to take shelter from a tornado, when warnings are given.

Joseph is an example of fleeing from an evil woman. (Genesis 39:7–23.) Daniel is an example of refusing to eat and drink anything harmful to the body. (Daniel 1:8–21.) Jesus is our perfect example. "For we have . . . one that hath been in all points tempted like as we are, yet without sin." (Hebrews 4:15.)

When Paul says flee from youthful lusts, in the same sentence, he tells young people what to do: follow after righteousness, faith, love, peace, with them that call on the Lord out of a pure heart. We can hardly get into trouble in that kind of company!

Do you like to go fishing? What kind of lure or bait do you use? Fishermen use many different kinds of bait according to what kind of fish they want to catch.

Temptation is very much like the bait on a hook. The fish does not see the hook, only that which appeals to or lures him. Remember the quotation from James? "Each man is tempted when he is drawn away by his own lust and enticed." Since each person has different tastes and desires, Satan has a bag of tricks to entice one.

Jesus won the victory over Satan in a threefold temptation by quoting scripture. He used the "Sword of the Spirit" (Ephesians 6:17), and so can you. Get acquainted with the wonderful words of wisdom in the Bible, especially Proverbs. Make a decision, with determination not to be lured into sin. Learn to say "no" and mean it.

WHEN TEMPTATION KNOCKS, ASK THE LORD TO GO TO THE DOOR FOR YOU, by quoting scripture.

Here are a few quotations you should memorize and be ready with the word of God on your lips.

"Abstain from every form of evil." (1 Thessalonians 4:22.)

"The drunkard and the glutton shall come to poverty." (Proverbs 23:21.)

"Lie not one to another." (Colossians 3:9.)

"Let another man praise thee, and not thine own mouth." (Proverbs 27:2.)

"Evil companionships corrupt good morals." (1 Corinthians 15:33.)

"If sinners entice thee, consent thou not." (Proverbs 1:10.)

When tempted to go to a dance, a swimming party (mixed bathing) or park on Lovers' Lane quote: "Can a man take fire in his bosom, and his clothes not be burned? Or can

one walk upon hot coals, and his feet not be scorched?"
(Proverbs 6:27, 28.)

When tempted to smoke tobacco, marijuana, use other drugs or drink alcoholic beverages, quote: "Know ye not that your body is a temple of the Holy Spirit which is in you, which ye have from God? and ye are not your own; for ye were bought with a price: glorify God therefore in your body." (1 Corinthians 6:19, 20.)

Willingness to accept responsibility is a sign of maturity. It is much easier to blame the other person for our mistakes. We can always ask God for help in making decisions. But God does not make us do right against our wills; neither can Satan make us do wrong against our wills.

> All the water in the world, however hard it tried,
> Could never, never sink a ship unless it got inside.
> All the evil in the world, the blackest kind of sin,
> Can never hurt you one least bit unless you let it in.

TO HELP IN MAKING DECISIONS REGARDING RIGHT OR WRONG.

THREE QUESTIONS
1. How will my participation in this activity affect me?
2. How will my participation in this activity affect others?
3. How will my participation in this activity affect the cause of Christ?

THREE TESTS
1. Test of secrecy. Would it be all right with me if everyone knew? Are there some specific individuals I would prefer not to know? Would I be embarrassed for mother to know? father? the preacher? elders?

2. Test of Prayer. Can I pray about this? Can I ask God to

be with me as I do this? What would Jesus do? What would Jesus have me do?

3. Test of universality. Would it be all right with me if everyone did this? Would it be O.K. for dad, mom, teacher, preacher, elders? What kind of a family, church, community, nation, world, would this be, if everyone did just like me?

THREE LIGHTS
WITHIN: Conscience, moral responsibility, common sense, knowledge.

WITHOUT: Other people, observation.

ABOVE: Study, prayer.

Topics For Discussion:

1. Abraham Lincoln and the Emancipation Proclamation.
2. How Lincoln's love of his dog portrayed character.
3. Our responsibility toward pets.
4. Quotation from Joseph Fort Newton.
5. Definition of decision.
6. A Christian's freedom.
7. Examples of using discretion (Proverbs 11:22.)
8. Difference in temptation and sin.
9. Two ways to deal with temptation.
10. Why we admire Joseph and Daniel.
11. How Jesus won the victory over Satan.
12. Proverbs that will help one overcome temptation.
13. I Corinthians 6:19, 20.
14. Deciding between right and wrong: three questions; three tests; three lights.

CHAPTER VI

Some Candid Camera Snap Shots

If I were doing a portrait of a young woman of the Bible, Ruth or Esther would be my choice. There is abundant material for a word picture or life size portrait of either person. Instead, some obscure personalities have been selected for snap shots.

The first snap shot is taken in Syria, of an unnamed maiden. She was only a servant girl in a strange land. Although we know nothing of her appearance, she had a beautiful spirit.

The king of Syria often sent his army into the land of Israel on raids. On one occasion, they captured a little maiden. Naaman, commander of the army of Benhadad, king of Damascus, gave the Hebrew girl to his wife as a servant.

When the little maid saw that Naaman was suffering from a dreadful disease, she said to her mistress: "Would that my lord were with the prophet that is in Samaria! then would he recover him of his leprosy."

There was no self pity nor bitterness because of her captivity. She made the best of her position. She did not forget God nor the true prophet in a foreign land. She also thought of the welfare of her captor. How unusual! It was because of her thoughtfulness that the king of Syria sent Naaman to Israel, where he was healed of his leprosy. (Story found in 2 Kings 5.)

The next snap shot is of the daughters of Shallum, taken in Jerusalem, while the walls were being rebuilt by Nehemiah, who had returned from captivity for that purpose. When work began, the wall was divided into different parts and important families were given a part to build. All the people were interested in helping. There were goldsmiths, perfumers and merchants working with the regular builders, such as masons and carpenters. Even the rulers worked diligently. From Nehemiah 3:12 we read "And next unto him repaired Shallum the son of Hallohesh, the ruler of half the district of Jerusalem, he and his daughters." They are the only women mentioned in this undertaking. We do not know how many daughters Shallum had, nor do we know their names, but we do know their disposition — "the people had a mind to work" is recorded in Nehemiah 4:6. When people make up their minds to complete a task, then nothing can stop them, even though enemies mocked and tried to stop the work. They prayed to God and set a watch day and night.

Every family was armed with swords, spears and bows. "And it came to pass from that time forth, that half of my servants wrought in the work, and half of them held the spears, the shields, and the bows, and the coats of mail; and the rulers were behind all the house of Judah. They that builded the wall and they that bare burdens laded themselves; every one with one of his hands wrought in the work, and with the other held his weapon; and the builders every one had his sword girded by his side, and so builded." (Nehemiah 4:16—18.) They worked from early morning till the stars appeared, even sleeping fully dressed, so the task was completed in fifty two days. (Nehemiah 6:15.)

The daughters of Shallum were mentioned in the record probably to show that although they belonged to a family of wealth and prestige they set an example of service. They were builders (construction workers) an unusual job for women, which took strength and courage.

In the month of May we honor our mothers on their day. A snap shot of Hannah is fitting at this time. She prayed for a son. (1 Samuel 1:11.) Vowing a vow, "Give unto thy handmaid a manchild, then I will give him unto Jehovah all the days of his life," in deep humility and sincerity.

God answered her prayer and gave her Samuel, whose name means "asked of God." Hannah was a consecrated mother who kept her vow at a great sacrifice. (1 Samuel 1:24–28; 2 Samuel 2:18.) She was willing to deny the joy of being with her child constantly so he could serve God. She was blessed with three other sons and two daughters. (1 Samuel 2:21.) Samuel grew up to be one of God's great prophets and blessed the whole nation. Our prayer is "Give us more mothers like Hannah!" (Proverbs 22:6; Ephesians 6:4.)

Our last snapshot is of a sorrowful mother. (2 Samuel 2:8–11.) Rizpah watched over the dead, unburied bodies of her two sons, beside the bodies of Saul's five grandsons. Her name has come to mean intense suffering, such as only a devoted mother can give.

We think of her counterpart today as all the mothers who sit at the bedside of sons or mourn the death of children who have been overcome with drugs or alcohol.

Rizpah's five month ordeal is one of literature's most tragic example of a mother's love. Our 20th century mothers who mourn (in sackcloth) of the wasted lives of children, who would not listen to words of wisdom and warning from the older generation, is also a tragic picture.

Things I wish I had Known

Having passed the first two score and ten years of my life, I find myself more prone to meditate and philosophize. My life has been rich, but there have been regrets. You too, will experience regrets in time. My regrets can largely be grouped as "Things I wish I had known before I was twenty-one."

I wish I had known:
1. What I was going to do for a living, and what my life work would likely be.
2. That my health after thirty was largely dependent on what I had put into my stomach before I was twenty-one.
3. How to take care of my money.
4. That a person's habits are mighty hard to change after twenty-one.
5. That the harvest depends upon the seeds sown.
6. That no one gets something for nothing.
7. That the world would give me just what I deserved.
8. The folly of not taking the advice of older and wiser people.
9. That Dad was not such an "old fogey" after all.
10. That everything Mother wanted me to do was right.
11. What it meant to my father and mother to raise a child.
12. More of the helpful and inspiring verses from the Bible.
13. The tremendous joy of serving another person.
14. That there is no better exercise for the heart than reaching down and helping people up.
15. That the "sweat of my brow" would earn my bread.
16. That a thorough education brings the best of everything else.
17. That honesty is the only policy, not only dealing with my neighbors, but also in dealing with myself and God.
18. The value of truthfulness in everything.

Today, I wish I had the formula for impressing you, young people, that life is a mirror which will reflect what you think about it.

Topics For Discussion:

1. Attitude of Hebrew maid in the house of her captor.
2. How the Hebrew maid showed her interest in Naaman's suffering.
3. Mission of Nehemiah.
4. Different classes of people who helped build the wall.
5. Daughters of Shallum and their father.
6. Hannah's prayer.
7. Hannah kept her vow at what sacrifice to herself.
8. Rizpah, a sorrowful mother.
9. Tragic examples of 20th Century mothers who mourn over wasted lives of their children.
10. Life is like a mirror.
11. Your own list of things to learn before age 21.

CHAPTER VII

High School Marriages

The following is copied from James W. Adams. "One of the manias of modern society is the craze to have too much too soon. The old virtue of waiting and working to obtain is obsolete. The precocious youth wants a hot-rod when he ought to be pedalling a bike. The young girl wants a boy friend when she ought to be playing with dolls. Young married people want a $30,000.00 ranch-style house in an elite suburb, when they should be living in a frame cottage on Thrift Avenue.

"High school boys and girls rush into the sacred institution of marriage and assume the responsibilities of household bills and children when they should be solving algebra problems and attending football games. There is a time for everything that is right and proper but nothing is made better by rushing into it. The divorce courts bear mute testimony to this truth with reference to marriage. How can the teenager who isn't ready to make a success of high school, think he is ready to make a success of marriage?

"Marriage is divinely ordained for man's good. It is hedged about by divine laws. It should not be entered inadvisedly or hurriedly, but in the fear of God. Christian young people should realize that marriage is UNTIL DEATH DO US PART. Divorce is not a part of the Christian's thinking. 'What God hath joined together, let not man put asunder' is the principle by which he lives. A relationship so sacred and permanent deserves mature consideration. Marriage was never designed to satisfy the whims and unrestrained desires of precocious infants."

Girls, if you are wearing a diamond ring or even thinking about getting engaged, use your head as well as your heart —

that is to say, use your intellect as well as your emotions. Next to becoming a Christian, marriage has more to do with the salvation of one's soul than anything else in life. The person you marry becomes a part of you. Therefore one should be very careful about the selection of a mate – the two become one flesh. The Christian girl is fastidious, not wishing to be joined in an intimate relationship with an immoral person. (1 Corinthians 6:13–20.) Ask yourself how a Christian can be one with a person who does not love God, his word and the church.

According to the Bible, love is the first consideration in marriage. If one takes the sacred marriage vows for money, convenience, sex, spite, or just to get away from home, unhappiness will follow. Faithfulness to marriage vows is based on our faithfulness to God and his word. Marry someone who can help you go to heaven. Read carefully and prayerfully the scriptures listed under obligations of marriage partners.

OBLIGATIONS OF MARRIAGE PARTNERS

(1 Corinthians 7:3–6; Colossians 3:18, 19; Ephesians 5:22, 23; 1 Peter 3:1–7.)

A. Husband

1. Love – to the degree that (a) Christ loved the church (enough to die for her.) (b) As he loves his own body. (Ephesians 5:25–33.)

2. Never bitter against her, because his strength and power are tempered with love and mercy. (Genesis 3:16b; Colossians 3:19.)

3. Honor, as weaker physically, which means support and protect. (1 Peter 3:7.) Failing to do so, his prayers are hindered.

B. Wife

1. Love (Titus 2:4.)

2. Be in subjection to, as the church, the bride of Christ; as a member of the body obeys the head; as Sarah obeyed Abraham, calling him lord. (Ephesians 5:22–24; 1 Peter 3:6.) Colossians 3:18: "Wives, be in subjection to your husbands, as is fitting in the Lord," teaches us that the wife is not to obey any command which would be contrary to the word of the Lord.

3. Reverence (fear, respect.) (Ephesians 5:33.) Why should it be offensive to respect and reverence the man one has chosen to be a life companion? Woman is in subjection, yes, but not to a stranger or an enemy, but to her husband, who loves her as Christ loves the church.

"As unto the bow the cord is
So unto the man is woman.
Though she bends him, she obeys him,
Though she draws him, yet she follows,
Useless each without the other."

— *Longfellow*
— *Song of Hiawatha*

Arrogance

Animals and inanimate objects speaking in fables can teach us many worth while lessons. The following story is an example.

A diamond found itself, to its extreme annoyance, lying

side by side with a piece of common blacklead under a gas jet. "Disgusting!" it remarked: "This is not fit society for a diamond of the first water." "Pooh!" said the blacklead carelessly, "you're only a bit of carbon like me," The diamond flashed furiously, "We are absolutely and fundamentally different," it said. "I have nothing in common with you, so be silent."

Presently, in came a chemist, with half a dozen pupils. "See here", he said, taking up the diamond and applying to it the full force of the blowpipe. To its horror, the diamond felt and saw itself swelling up into a horrible blackmass before resolving into an invisible and noxious gas. As it faded away, its last recognized sensation was a malicious gleam emanating from the blacklead. The rich and proud too often regard themselves as diamonds, and forget that in the GREAT CHEMIST'S furnace they will prove to be of the same elements as the poor and humble.

The wise man Solomon, describes the arrogance of the diamond and of people who have that attitude: "Before destruction the heart of man is haughty; and before honor goes humility." (Proverbs 18:12.) No person can really achieve greatness and honor in this life until one has first humbled himself. If one has a haughty spirit, it will surely be one's destruction.

Paul admonishes a Christian in Romans 12:3: "Not to think of himself more highly than he ought to think: BUT SO TO THINK AS TO THINK SOBERLY." Every person must know his own ability. To you it means not to over-estimate yourself, or to under-estimate your talents, but to think soberly or seriously about your real capacity. Then you will never be inflated by flattery or "put down" by criticism.

For instance suppose you are a singer. Your friends may

praise you to the skies and insist that you should start recording your songs. In their estimation you will have a gold record in no time! Your critics may say you are no good at all! But you can think soberly if your teachers say you have the capacity to become a famous singer, and you are willing to spend money, time and energy, then do it! In Ecclesiastes 9:10 we read: "Whatsoever thy hand findeth to do, do it with thy might." But my advice is to be wise enough to know what not to attempt.

Paul gives further instruction: "Set not your mind on high things, but condescend to things that are lowly." (Romans 12:16.) In another letter (2 Corinthians 10:12) Paul discusses those who commend themselves too highly. "But they themselves measuring themselves by themselves, an comparing themselves with themselves, are without understanding." Remember the parable of the Pharisee and the Publican. (Luke 18:9–14.) Jesus said: "For every one that exalteth himself shall be humbled; but he that humbleth himself shall be exalted."

Calling Evil Good

Here is a message from Isaiah that is needed.

"Woe unto them that call evil good, and good evil; that put darkness for light, and light for darkness; that put bitter for sweet, and sweet for bitter!" (Isaiah 5:20.)

Today this woe is pronounced on all who advertise alcoholic beverages in attractive ways, with orchids, roses and beautiful ladies. Billboards on the highways, TV programs and the movies all have a tendency to make drinking glamorous. They are calling evil good and trying to persuade young people that it is smart to drink beer and wine.

There is an effort to appeal to the home maker to serve more beer and wine at home. They offer to supply recipes and menus in the ads. One claim made is that beer is non-fattening and a new taste thrill! The idea is not so much in getting people to drink more beer, but in getting more people to drink beer.

The highly colored and brightly lighted signboards would make one believe that bitter is sweet, darkness is light, and evil is good. Let us remember Proverbs 1:10: "If sinners entice thee, consent thou not."

The Bible is full of warnings against strong drink, such as: gin, ale, vodka, whiskey and wine. Strong drink causes poverty and suffering; is a deadly poison, and takes away the understanding. Not only does the Bible teach against it, but medical men and scientists do.

Dr. Charles Mayo said: "You can get along with a wooden leg, but you can't get along with a wooden head. In order that your brain may be kept clear, you must keep your body fit and well. That can not be done if one drinks liquor."

It was reported to the American Association for the Advancement of Science, a few years ago, by a group of Harvard students, that alcohol's effect on the human brain, as recorded by electrical instruments, is a cross between sleep and suffocation.

What do we think of persons who ignore such signs: on the highway, "CAUTION, BRIDGE OUT"; at a gateway, "BEWARE THE DOG"; at the beach, "UNSAFE FOR SWIMMING – SHARKS"; at camp, on the woodland trails, "WATCH FOR SNAKES (copperheads and rattlers.)"?

In Proverbs 23:31 we read: "Look not thou upon the wine when it is red, when it sparkleth in the cup, when it goeth down smoothly: at the last it biteth like a serpent, and stingeth like an adder."

We would never stoop to pick a lovely flower, if we knew a poisonous snake was hiding there. We are told that fish are smarter than men, sometimes, when they refuse to take the bait on the hook.

COUNSEL FOR YOUTH

Son, these are thoughts to remember,
    and check against every device:
Will the pleasure you're tempted to purchase prove costly
    or cheap at the price?
The thing which for nothing is offered, is merely the bait
    on a hook,
Whenever you're prompted to take it, on all sides make
    certain to look.

– Edgar A. Guest

At banquets or dinners, or at any social function, never be tempted to drink because everyone else is doing so. It is not impolite for guests to refuse certain foods because they are on a diet. Neither is it being impolite to your hostess to refuse alcoholic beverages because of your conscience.

Resolve to always say, "No, thank you," when alcoholic drinks are passed anywhere and you will be wise. It was Shakespeare who said. "O, that men would put an enemy into their mouths, to steal away their brains!"

Perhaps this is why Solomon says, "Wine is a mocker, strong drink a brawler; and whosoever erreth thereby is not wise." To mock is to disappoint the hopes of; tantalize; make sport of. Therefore, it is wise never to take the first drink. Only a foolish person will begin such a loathsome habit, which will ruin his life on earth and cause him to be lost eternally. No drunkard can inherit the kingdom of heaven.

This story is told about William Penn, who was advising a man to stop drinking. "Can you tell me how to do it?" asked the slave of the drinking habit. "Yes," answered Penn, "It is just as easy as to open the hand, friend." The man replied: "Convince me of that, and I will promise upon my honor to do as you tell me." Said the good Quaker, "Well, my friend, when thou findest any vessel of intoxicating liquor in thy hand, open the hand that grasps it, before it reaches thy mouth, and thou wilt never be drunk again."

The Cigarette Speaks

I'm just a friendly cigarette,
Don't be afraid of me!
Why, all the advertisers say I'm harmless as can be.
They tell you that I'm your best friend
(I like that cunning lie),
And say that you'll walk a mile for me
Because I satisfy!

So, come on, girlie, be a sport,
Why longer hesitate?
With me between your pretty lips
You'll be quite up-to-date!
You may not like me right at first,
But very soon I'll bet
You'll find you can't get along
Without a cigarette!

You've smoked one pack, so now I know
I have no cause to fear;
When once I get a grip on girls,
They're mine for life, my dear.
Your freedom you began to lose
The very day we met,
When I convicned you it was smart
To smoke a cigarette.

The color's fading from your cheeks,
Your fingertips are stained;
And now you'd like to give me up
But, sister, you are chained!
You even took a drink last night —
I thought you would ere long.
For those whom I enslave soon lose
Their sense of right and wrong.

Year after year, I've fettered you
And led you blindly on,
"til you're now just a bunch of nerves
With looks and health both gone.
You're pale and thin, and have a cough —
The doctor says "TB".
He says you can't expect to live
Much longer, thanks to me!

But it's too late to worry now;
When you become my slave
You should have known the chances were
You'd find an early grave.

And now that I have done my best
To send your soul to hell,
I'll leave you with my partner, Death,
He's come for you, Farewell!
                                    — *Author Unknown*

Topics For Discussion:

1. The two things in life that have more to do with the salvation of our souls than anything else.
2. Manias of modern society.
3. The first marriage. Why God ordained marriage.
4. Why take time to choose a life companion.
5. Why faithfulness to marriage vows is based on faithfulness to God and his word.
6. Obligations of marriage partners.
7. Conversation of diamond and blacklead.
8. How a chemist changed the situation. The Great Chemist's furnace.
9. How Romans 12:13 helps us to deal with flattery or criticism.
10. Meaning of Luke 18:14b.
11. Apply Isaiah 5:20 to our times.
12. Quotation from Dr. Charles Mayo.
13. Harvard students' report of effect of alcohol on human brain.
14. Signs we do not ignore.
15. How wine is a mocker.
16. William Penn's story.
17. What the cigarette says to me.

CHAPTER VIII

Rules For Christian Living

All rules for Christian living are based on love. It is love for God that caused us to become Christians in the first place. Love must guide us in our treatment of other people if we want to please the Lord. "Love suffereth long, and is kind." (1 Corinthians 13:4.) Kind means to be good natured and gentle; the opposite of bad tempered and rude.

When one really loves another person there is a desire to make that one happy. Therefore, the Christian, who loves all people, will be polite and courteous toward all. Being polite is being kind. A good motto for both old and young people is: "Be ye kind." A motto is a guiding rule of conduct. Someone has said that love is kindness at work.

It is good to read often the famous Sermon on the Mount to learn the teaching of Jesus about how to treat others. "But I say unto you that hear, Love your enemies, do good to them that hate you, bless them that curse you, pray for them that despitefully use you." (Luke 6:27, 28.)

An enemy is a person that is hostile or unfriendly toward another. Has anyone ever mistreated you? Perhaps you could not love one who has wronged you as you love your mother or your best friend. The love Jesus commands us to have for enemies will cause us to do them good. Paul wrote the Roman Christians: "If thine enemy hunger, feed him; if he thirst, give him to drink: for in so doing thou shalt heap coals of fire upon his head." (Romans 12:20.) By returning good for evil, the one in the wrong can be made ashamed of himself. "Render to no man evil for evil . . . if it be possible, as much as in you lieth, be at peace with all men." (Romans 12:17, 18.)

Christians should not punish their enemies. God will do it for them. Not only on the judgment day will he do this, but by the laws of the land. The police take care of public enemies,' such as robbers, murderers and all other law breakers. (Romans 13:1—7.) It is right to seek protection of life and property by calling on officers of the law.

"To him that smiteth thee on the one cheek offer also the other; and from him that taketh away thy cloak withold not thy coat also. Give to every one that asketh thee; and of him that taketh away thy goods ask them not again. And as ye would that men should do to you, do ye also to them likewise." (Luke 6:29—31.)

In the common, every day affairs of life, when someone tries to start a fight, don't fight back. It takes two to make a quarrel. It is better to suffer wrong than to do wrong. The Golden Rule helps us to decide what to say and do when people try to take advantage of us.

It helps me to have the right attitude when I read these words of Jesus: "But love your enemies, and do them good, and lend, never despairing; and your reward shall be great, and ye shall be sons of the Most High: for he is kind toward the unthankful and evil. Be ye merciful, even as your Father is merciful." (Luke 6:35, 36.) If we want to be children of our heavenly Father, we must be kind and merciful, remembering there is a reward.

"And judge not, and ye shall not be judged; and condemn not, and ye shall not be condemned; release, and ye shall be released; give and it shall be given unto you; good measure, pressed down, shaken together, running over, shall they give into your bosom. For with what measure ye mete it shall be measured to you again." (Luke 6:37, 38.)

Judging is the opposite of showing mercy. To be unfair

in forming an opinion of others is the judging that is forbidden. We have been taught to judge a tree by the fruit it bears. Good people do good things and evil people do evil things. If we are unselfish and kind toward others, they will treat us the same way. Life is like a mirror. Smile and a smile will be reflected. Frown and see what happens. "Give to the world the best you have, and the best will come back to you." It takes a Christian to do good to all men. He tries to be like God, who is kind toward the unthankful and evil.

Air Castles

Dreams? Yes, day dreams, those little bits of nothing, so full of meaning. Dreams are only pretty thoughts and ambitions, but often they grow and fill a whole life. Dreams – ah . . . this imaginative world is a beautiful place to live in. One might have a shack for a home, and still dwell in a palace of golden dreams. Castles in the air can be with you always. No person can be deprived of intimate fancies. Blow pretty bubbles! If they burst, that's all right. The next will be more lovely than the last.

Why waste time with day dreams? What can they amount to? They give vent to emotions stored up that otherwise, seemingly, cannot be expressed. A person can really make his dreams come true. He can put the foundations under castles in the air. One may ask, "What if one fails?" Well, just be thankful, it was of air and not brick and stone, so that when it tumbled, no harm was done. Just get busy and construct another castle more exquisite than the first. All of the old material goes into the new one, mixed with later impressions and sentiments. An individual truly reveals his character by dreams, aspirations and hopes.

A mother dreams and plans for the future of her child. She makes for him a career, where he will achieve fame and riches, in her dreams. Oftentimes a mother's ideals save a boy from destruction. She has held up before her son the ideal of life and manhood. She has created the character she wants him to be and engraved it on his heart. Solomon told us how to do this: "Train up a child in the way he should go, And even when he is old he will not depart from it." (Proverbs 22:6.)

Young women, early in life, build castles in the air. Girls, as you well know, are romance loving creatures. What girl does not dream of "Prince Charming" in many shapes and forms? She dreams of a gallant love, handsome and true. Every trait that is noble and great she adds to her dream and unconsciously builds her Ideal Man. She keeps the imaginary Prince constantly in her mind and compares him to every man she meets. Finally, one does come on the scene that measures up to the standard, or nearly so. (They say love is blind.) Then, one little castle in the air is completed before it tumbled — a dream come true.

Young men in truth can be said to "Hitch their wagons to a star." They too can soar in flights of fancy. A farmer boy slips away to fish on the quiet banks of a creek, just to be alone and dream, gazing up into the blue sky, watching the clouds go sailing by. Another boy sits on the beach and looks far out to sea. The waves all have a tale to tell him and he listens as he weaves his dreams.

A study of great men and women in history has inspired many young people to dream of the future, (especially great Bible characters!)

"Lives of great men all remind us we can make our lives sublime", said Longfellow. If a person dreams long enough and earnestly enough, he can become great. It is a matter of putting something real under the castle in the air, a good, strong corner stone for instance, so that the structure will stand. We dream and plan, then we work and execute the plan. It is not only probably, but really possible to make a dream come true.

Old people like to be alone sometimes, just to reflect. "Build thee more stately mansions O my soul as the swift seasons roll." At twilight, a very old man and his wife sit side by side watching the shadows fall. The firelight softens the wrinkles in their kindly faces, as they dream. They talk of their many, many castles in the air and what these castles have meant to them. Some of the castles have vanished long ago, others stand secure. "Not failure, but low aim is crime" said the old man. His wife replied: "A man's reach should exceed his grasp, or what's a heaven for?" They are contented and happy because of lives well spent. Their dreams were worth while.

"For in the multitude of dreams there are vanities, and in many words: but fear thou God." (Eccl. 5:7.)

The Sweet Girl Graduate
(From diapers to cap and gown in 18 years.)

She made her advent into the world at E.C.M. Hospital, February 24, 1960, a blue-eyed, brown-haired living doll, where grandmothers, grandfathers, aunts, uncles and many friends of the family formed a receiving line in front of the nursery window. The young mother smiled through a mass of red roses, ferns and pink hyacinths, from her hospital bed, while the young father, in a daze, passed out cigars of pink bubble gum, with this inscription: IT'S A GIRL. All of the relatives and friends were excited about extending a warm welcome to the new baby, but she just looked bored and yawned.

What is a baby? Here are some thought provoking definitions: a padlock on the chain of love. The most extensive employer of female labor. The only precious possession that never excites envy. A stranger with unspeakable cheek, that enters a house without a stitch to its back and is received with open arms by everybody. About twenty-two inches of coo and wiggle, writhe and scream, filled with suction and testing apparatus for milk, and automatic alarm to regulate supply. That which makes home happier, love stronger, patience greater, hands busier, nights longer, days shorter, purses lighter, the future brighter.

Infants do grow. This one became a terrible toddler, who liked to be front center on the family stage — a real ham, when the audience gave rapt attention to her cute antics. Unfortunately, there was someone else in the family who would like to thrust her out of the spotlight. The threat came from the menacing form of Big Brother, who was taller and stronger. Little sister developed methods of counter attack, such as biting and scratching. It is comforting to know that through it all, they loved each other dearly. Just when the little one was learning to defend herself, she began to be taught about sharing. This idea of getting along with people became a part of growing up, making friends with a circle of play-mates. At this age, she began to be aware that God was a near relation, included in all plans.

The next period of her life was one of "Sugar and Spice and Everything Nice." Dolls dominated her existence. She played and slept with rag dolls, walking and talking dolls, a Tubsy and a Barbie doll. Many of these dolls lost their hair as she practiced her beautician's art in giving permanents, shampoos changing color, or what have you!

Falls from tricycles and bikes never seemed to matter very much as she went on her merry way. Wheels were not her "thing." Various interests claimed her attention, however. At five years of age she was Queen of the Tigers, a soft ball team, and Valentine Queen in the second grade. She was growing in the social graces.

At an early age she learned to swim. Her grandmother feared that she would sprout fins and become a kind of water animal, because she liked the water so much. Water skiis were a natural. She became quite proficient in water sports. The family had a place on Pickwick lake, where they spent vacations. This was just about her favorite spot on earth.

There was never a girl who loved animals any more as pets: stray kittens, puppies and finally a pedigreed poodle, Tony. One of the pets was named "Punch," whom she took with her one time to visit her grandmother. The pup was not invited in the house, but asked to stay on the porch, much to the displeasure of a certain little girl. Punch was insulted and showed it by barking and scratching at the door during the visit. Grandmother had a change of heart. The very next morning, she put this note in the mail: "Dear One: I realize that pet owners say, 'Love me; love my dog.' Forgive me please. Next time you come to see me, bring Punch and he will be welcome, fleas and all! Love, Grandmother."

For a time, all of her affection was lavished on horses. She collected pictures and statuettes of horses. Every available space in her room was filled with such keepsakes. One might get the impression that this was a stable instead of a bedroom. Her very own gentle horse was named Penney. Her brother owned Star and her Colt, Stan's Twinkle. Many happy hours were spent barrel racing and trail riding with the cousins, who also had their won horses.

Our girl wore a permanent sun tan, because she loved the

out-of-doors. She delighted in being a Brownie and enjoyed their activities. Volley ball was a favorite game. She played soft ball on a team named "The Chicks" for three summers. During junior high school years she was a cheer leader for the basket ball team at her school.

There were also interesting indoor activities. Piano lessons were counted as important for a few years. Learning to sew was exciting because it meant new clothes. Crewel embroidery was a passing fad. A pretty design on a shirt or a pair of blue jeans was a must. She even spent hours making her brother a fancy jacket. Some of her hobbies were ceramics, decoupage and macrame. Baby sitting for family friends was an after school job occasionally. Boy friends were changed as often as the current records of favorite songs. However, a host of intimate girl friends constantly surrounded her. Slumber parties were a week-end special! Woe unto the mother whose house was chosen for the giggling party!

Wearing braces on her teeth was something to be endured. She hated it, but it did improve her appearance. Later she appreciated the fact that someone cared enough to see that her teeth were straightened. She became a lovely, attractive girl, chosen as an attendant in the Queen's court for homecoming in the 10th grade. She was really pleased to be selected as president of her class that year, considering it an honor. During the next few years she served as bridesmaid in weddings of close friends.

In the early teens, she went through a temperamental, independent stage, but she was really a cooperative, pleasant person. Not only did she help with the chores at home, but enjoyed working on the bus at church. She served as assistant Sunday School teacher for a nursery class for several years, and related well to the small children. One summer she had an opportunity to work in a gospel campaign in the Caribbean

Islands which she enjoyed. Attending youth meetings, workshops and retreats was a regular routine.

During the last two years in high school, she decided to study Cosmetology in Vocational school, in order to learn certain skills, preparatory to a professional career. Her ambition proved to be a worthy one. With hard work and native ability she has won the following trophies, medals and medallions.

1. Medallion — second place World's Fair of Beauty (hair cutting) student competition, in Tennessee.

2. Trophy — first place in Burrell-Slater VICA hair fashion show.

3. Trophy — first place in Vocational Industrial Clubs of America Cosmetology district contest.

4. Gold medal — as number one Cosmetology student in Alabama.

5. Third place — representing Alabama in the VICA Skills Olympics National. She also received a scholarship as an outstanding student in Vocational School. Thanks to her good teachers, she is beginning to realize some of her dreams.

The above fancies and foibles of a typical southern girl, reared in a Christian environment, describe to a limited degree, my beloved granddaughter.

Grace is deceitful, and beauty is vain,
But a woman that feareth Jehovah, she shall be praised.
Give her of the fruit of her hands;
And let her works praise her in the gates.
  (Proverbs 31:30, 31.)

Topics For Discussion:

1. Basis of all rules for Christian living.
2. How to love enemies.
3. Why Christians do not punish their enemies.
4. Who takes care of public enemies.
5. Better to suffer wrong than to do wrong.
6. Kind of judging forbidden to Christians.
7. Making dreams come true by hard work.
8. Activities of a typical southern girl in a Christian environment.
9. Apply Proverbs 31:30, 31.

CHAPTER IX

A Default Caused By Onions

Girls, this is a short story about a happening in the life of a young girl. It could be called a parable. You remember of course, that Jesus used common, ordinary objects and things as: a plow, a fish net, birds, grass, lilies of the field, to teach us lessons.

Many years ago when I was a speech teacher, my students often entered contests. It was a great day when one of my girls brought home a gold medal from a state tournament. It caused great rejoicing at school.

The next year, a girl just as talented, entered a contest promoted by The Birmingham News, for all interested students in our state. Every contestant spoke on one phase of the life of Abraham Lincoln. All members of my class were encouraged to prepare a speech, which they did. The best entry went to the county contest. The winner was an attractive girl, outstanding in scholastic attainments, with some experience in dramatics. She had poise and a good voice, along with her intelligence. To my way of thinking, she was TOPS and would bring honor to her school.

The talented winner from our school had something else on her mind in addition to making a speech. Since she was to compete away from home, she wanted a new dress and new shoes. Her ambition was to make a good appearance on the stage.

It was easy to get a new dress — her mother could sew. She eagerly assumed a few extra chores about the house, so mother could have time to make a lovely dress. It seems there was a lack of funds to buy the expensive shoes she so much wanted. Her father told her if she would gather the onions in the garden, tie them in bunches to sell, she could have the money. At once she began the task, working after school. However it was a bigger job than she anticipated, taking both time and energy. When the onions were ready, they must be carried to market. Then of course, there was a shopping trip for the beautiful shoes, just right for the occasion.

Perhaps you can guess that the story has a sad ending. The last days before the contest, our little lady was not calmly polishing her speech, but she was rushing around in a frenzy of anxiety. Although she was probably the prettiest and best dressed girl on the stage, the Judges of the contest did not select her as the winner. Her speech material was excellent, but the final preparation was lacking.

It is necessary to be well groomed for a public appearance, but the delivery of a good speech should have been the first consideration. Yes, the young lady learned an important lesson. Can you profit from this story by putting first things first?

Honesty

Young Friends — think with me on the theme of Honesty. Definition: fairness and straight forwardness in speech, conduct and thought. Free from fraud or deceit; open and frank.
— *Webster*

We all remember Diogenes, the Greek, who went about the streets of Athens with a lighted lantern, in the middle of the day, seeking for an honest man.

From Jeremiah 5:1 we have a similar incident: "Run ye to and fro through the streets of Jerusalem, and see now, and know, and seek in the broad places thereof, if ye can find a man, if there be any that doeth justly, that speaketh truth; and I will pardon her."

There is nothing more important, and few things more difficult, than to be honest and really love the truth. Few crimes are committed without the motive of dishonesty.

Honesty in people means you can predict their actions and dishonesty means they are evasive and unpredictable. The only way to be honest is to love the truth and love God. Luke 8:4—5 relates the parable of the sower. Verse 15 is impressive: "And that in the good ground, these are such as in an honest and good heart, having heard the word, hold it fast, and bring forth fruit with patience." The seed sown in the good ground was the word of God and we know "Thy word is truth." May we not reach this conclusion? A person can not receive God's word, the truth, without an honest heart. An honest and good heart is the foundation of Christian character.

With these thoughts in mind, I want to share the following clipping. Ann Landers likes to have her column quoted by religious teachers.

Dear Ann Landers: The letter from the mother whose son was selling his homework prompted me to write.

I am a teacher who has had considerable experience with cheaters. The student who believes he can copy homework and get away with it is stupid. It is easy for a teacher to discern which student prepared the original work and which student copied it.

At the beginning of each semester, I announce that any

student who copies or allows his work to be copied will automatically get an F. I then hand out a memo so there will be no misunderstanding. This has virtually eliminated cheating in my classes. Of course, a few smarties have to test me, but they soon discover I mean business. Print this if you like, but no name or city, please.

Dear Teacher: Thanks for your letter and the attached memo which I would like to reprint.

MEMO TO THOSE WHO ALLOW THEIR WORK TO BE COPIED:

You are cheating the person who copies. If he fails to do his assignment, he does not learn. If he does not learn he can not do well on his exam. Are you being fair to him?

You are cheating the classmate who has not done his assignment, but is honest enough to admit it. This person, though unprepared, is at least assuming responsibility for himself. Are you being fair to him?

You are taking a chance on being found out and receiving an F. Are you being fair to yourself?

MEMO TO THOSE WHO COPY FROM OTHERS:

You are cheating the person who has done the work. If he gets caught he gets an F. Are you being fair to him?

You are cheating the classmate who has not done his work but is honest enough to take responsibility for himself. Are you being fair to him?

You are not getting the benefit of learning, nor will you be able to pass the exam when the time comes. Are you being fair to yourself?

Let's Go Shopping

The ancient Greeks defined woman as "an animal fond of dress." Even now in the twentieth century, the fair sex is still interested in high fashion. What clothing to wear has been a topic of discussion in all generations. There are many faithful women who like to be well dressed when they appear in public and at the same time be well pleasing to the Lord. Sometimes a real problem confronts us when the time comes to purchase clothing for women and girls in a family. Whether one shops for fabrics and patterns or ready-made garments, decisions have to be made as to what is in good taste and proper for a Christian.

The Bible was written for all people, in every country and climate, for every century as long as time lasts. The Holy Spirit has given us a message that each generation can understand and apply to every day living. Human nature is the same from Adam to us. Customs change but principles of righteousness do not change. Does the Bible give us information as to how to shop for a new dress? Yes, it does.

CLOTHING INDICATES CHARACTER, AS WELL AS POSITION, we may learn from the following passages:

1. Garments of widowhood. (Genesis 38:14, 15.)

2. The attire of a harlot. (Proverbs 7:10.)

3. Priest's garments, made for "glory and for beauty;" (Exodus 28:40.) also for modesty (Exodus 28:42.)

4. Garments of divers colors for king's daughters and virgins. (2 Samuel 13:18, 19.)

5. Jezebel. (2 Kings 9:30—37.)

6. The worthy woman had a love for the beautiful and practical; warm clothes for the family; beautiful tapestry

for the home; purple and fine linen for herself, which she could afford because of her station in life. (Proverbs 31:21, 22.)

7. Vashti, the queen. (Esther 1:10—12.) Was she deposed because of modesty?

8. Daughters of Zion "are haughty and walk with out-stretched necks and wanton eyes." (Isaiah 3:16—26.) Read this description of their costumes and accessories.

9. John the Baptist wore the simple clothing of the prophets, instead of "soft raiment." (Matthew 3:4; 11:8, 9.)

10. The demoniac, when healed by Jesus was "clothed and in his right mind." (Luke 8:26—39.)

IS IT WRONG FOR CHRISTIAN WOMEN TO WEAR BEAUTIFUL CLOTHING? Let the apostle Paul answer the question. Quoting from 1 Timothy 2:9, 10: "In like manner, that women adorn themselves in modest apparel, with shamefacedness and sobriety; not with braided hair, and gold or pearls or costly raiment; but (which becometh women professing godliness) through good works."

The word adorn defined by Webster means to "beautify, dignify; ornament, embellish." James McKnight says: "The Greek word adorn signifies not only what is beautiful, but what is neat and clean, and suitable to one's station." To be properly dressed is to be well groomed. "A female may as truly violate the precepts of her religion by neglecting her personal appearance as by excessive attention to it." —Albert Barnes. One extreme is as bad as another. The Christian does not decorate herself like a Christmas tree, for show and ornamentation. On the other hand, she is not a barefoot sloven, with disheveled hair, wearing dirty, ragged garments.

It seems to be requisite that Christian women adorn or beautify themselves in becoming apparel, in order to be as lovely and attractive as possible. Each individual should study colors, lines, materials and designs best suited for her garments and have them fitted properly. She owes it to herself to look her best, because clothing should reflect the personality of an individual.

DRESS IS TO A PERSON, WHAT A FRAME IS TO A PICTURE. A well dressed woman is one whose costume is so rightly designed that one remembers her charming personality and not what she wore. Therefore, it is the responsibility of the Christian woman to use her ingenuity in modifying modern styles and patterns to conform to God's standards. Accept any good ideas presented by designers from Paris or Hollywood and reject the bad ones, remembering that Christians are in the world but not "of the world."

SELECTING A MODEST DRESS ON OUR SHOPPING TOUR. Besides adornment, there are other considerations in selecting a wardrobe for the Christian woman. Quoting "with shamefacedness and sobriety." The word modest means: "Restrained by a due sense of propriety; diffident; decent; chaste." The word propriety means: "Conforming to established rules or customs; fitness; decorum." Decent means: "Becoming; respectable; modest."

Now let us define the phrase: "With shamefacedness and sobriety." Scholars tell us shamefacedness is that which is made fast by an honorable shame. The word sobriety as used here means "sanity." It can also mean soberness, moderation of the desires and passions. It is opposed to all that is frivolous, and to all undue excitement of the passions. A Christian woman, of sound mind, is therefore ashamed to appear in public in indecent garments. We remember the story of Bathsheba. (2 Samuel 11:2.) Also the teaching of Jesus in Matthew 5:27. A Christian woman would never want to dress or undress in such a manner as to cause others to be guilty of adultery. We are told to put on apparel, adorn oneself, not to leave off clothing!

The price of clothing is important to a Christian. "Costly raiment" is perhaps a relative term. Clothing is too expensive if one spends beyond one's income. Perhaps the same garment would not be too costly for a wealthy person in a high position in life. Ordinary people do not dress as a governor's wife or the president's wife, when they represent our government, as an illustration. Money spent for clothing that should have been used for more important things, also makes the garment too costly.

JESUS' TEACHING ABOUT CLOTHING. (Matthew 6:25—34.) Jesus said: "for your heavenly Father knoweth that ye have need of all these things" — (food, shelter and clothing) — an excerpt from The Sermon on the Mount. Read the verses carefully and you will learn that seeking Christ and his Kingdom is of primary importance. To spend all of our time, money and energy on feeding and clothing the body is vanity, waste of time and un-Christian.

PAUL'S TEACHING ABOUT CLOTHING. (1 Timothy 2:9, 10.) We have commented on verse 9. Now in verse 10 Paul stresses GOOD WORKS AS THE CHIEF ADORNMENT OF GODLY WOMEN.

PETER'S TEACHING TO THE CHRISTIAN WIFE. (1 Peter 3:1—6.)

THE INWARD ADORNING OF A BEAUTIFUL CHARACTER IS STRESSED.

Topics For Discussion:

1. The importance of being well groomed for a public appearance.
2. The importance of a good speech in a contest.
3. Priorities — first things first.
4. Definition of honesty.
5. Foundation of Christian character.
6. Memo to those who allow their work to be copied.
7. Memo to those who copy from others.
8. How clothing indicates character.
9. Meaning of word adorn.
10. Meaning of word modest.
11. When clothing is too costly.
12. Jesus' teaching on clothing.
13. Paul's teaching on clothing.
14. Peter's teaching on clothing.

CHAPTER X

Heart Portraits

The second Sunday in May every year we honor our mothers. What a privilege. If our own mother has departed to the "land beyond the grave," then we can adopt a lonely mother, who has no children with her anymore and make her feel loved and needed. Is that not what Mother's Day is all about?

Mother is the Bible's most honored woman. The word mother is used almost three hundred times. In the Old Testament, Sarah, Jochebed, Hannah and Ruth are great mothers. A study of the lives of these great women makes us realize what they have contributed to the history of God's people. I have been impressed with another group of women in Old Testament history, the mothers of the kings of Judah.

The following quotation is from "All of the Women of the Bible," by Edith Deen: "Right after the names of queen-mothers in Kings and Chronicles, there usually occurs a phrase summarizing the spiritual and moral tone of the king's reign 'and he did that which was right in the sight of the Lord' or 'and he did that which was evil in the sight of the Lord.' The juxtaposition of the queen-mother's name and an evaluation of her son's reign seems significant."

Yes, we can agree that such expressions are full of meaning. The influence of a mother can be very good or very bad, not only in the life of a king, but on any child. In Ezekiel 16:44 we read, "As is the mother, so is her daughter." Example is a very powerful influence.

In the New Testament we read of an outstanding young preacher, named Timothy. Paul's comments about him were: "I sent unto you Timothy, who is my beloved and faithful child in the Lord." (1 Corinthians 4:17.) "For he worketh the work of the Lord, as I also do." (1 Corinthians 16:10.)

To the Philippians Paul wrote: "But I hope in the Lord Jesus to send Timothy shortly unto you, that I also may be of good comfort, when I know your state. For I have no man likeminded, who will care truly for your state. For they all seek their own, not the things of Jesus Christ. But ye know the proof of him, that, as a child serveth a father, so he served with me in furtherance of the gospel." (Phil. 2: 19—22.)

Why was Timothy such a great young preacher? Paul tells us in a letter to him. "Having been reminded of the unfeigned faith that is in thee; which dwelt first in thy grandmother Lois, and thy mother Eunice; and I am persuaded in thee also." (2 Timothy 1:5.) Paul also said ". . . he served with me in furtherance of the gospel." (Philippians 2:19—22.)

2 Timothy 3:14, 15 gives this exhortation, "But abide thou in the things which thou has learned and hast been assur - ed of, knowing of whom thou hast learned them; and that from a babe thou hast known the sacred writings which are able to make thee wise unto salvation through faith which is in Christ Jesus."

There could never have been a Timothy without a Lois and a Eunice! These godly women taught their child the word of God, as a babe in arms. They had great faith and imparted it to their son, who was then ready to be taught of Paul and preach the gospel to many people.

We need more grandmothers and mothers like Lois and Eunice who can produce gospel preachers. It is not in the colleges and universitities that young men always receive inspiration to carry out the Great Commission. The home is more often responsible for giving a youngster the desire to proclaim the good news.

On Mother's Day it is good to be reminded of a very touching scene in the life of our Lord. As he hung on the cross, he thought of his mother. Not wishing for her to comfort him, alleviate his pain and suffering, but in this dark hour of death, burdened with all the sins of the whole world, he was thinking of his mother's welfare — providing a home for her with the beloved John, who would love and care for her. "When Jesus therefore saw his mother, and the disciple standing by whom he loved, he saith unto his mother, Woman, behold, thy son! Then saith he to the disciple, Behold, thy mother! And from that hour the disciple took her unto his own home." (John 19:26.) Jesus taught us this wonderful lesson: NOT WHAT MOTHER CAN DO FOR ME: BUT WHAT CAN I DO FOR MOTHER.

HEART PORTRAITS
By Kathryn Lawyer Deveney

Three women stood, in morning's hush,
    Beside the tomb.
And chirped a thrush
    From yonder olive tree.

Sighed one, "He was my friend."
    The second said, "He was my Lord."
The third wept quietly,
    "He was my son," said she.

A Hemorrhage Of The Mouth

Solomon the wise man said: "The foolish woman is clamorous; she is simple and knoweth nothing." (Proverbs 9:13.) Who wants to be silly and ignorant? Rather we desire to be charming and sophisticated as we grow into womanhood. One's actions make known to the world the real personality. Loud boistrous talking, laughing and giggling in public places could easily brand a person as foolish; one who is uninformed and ignorant in matters of good breeding. Thinking determines actions; actions determine attitudes; and attitudes determine character.

It was also Solomon who said: "In the multitude of words there wanteth not transgression: but he that refraineth his lips doeth wisely." (Proverbs 10:19.) Incessant chattering is not a virtue. It is a known fact that one who talks constantly will get into trouble by telling more than one knows or by "stretching the truth." Repeating rumors or gossip is dangerous. It is a wise person who knows when to be silent. Dr. Dooley, of the Cumberland mountains, in Tennessee often was heard to quote: "Some people have a hemorrhage of the mouth that can not be stopped."

"Study to be quiet, and to do your own business, and to work with your hands, even as we charged you" (1 Thessalonian 4:11.), Paul advised the Thessalonian Christians. It takes a little study, both thinking and self control, to be quiet. Tend to your own business is good advice. Never meddle in the affairs of others. Keeping busy helps one to avoid the temptation. "The meek and quiet spirit which is in the sight of God of great price" (1 Peter 3:4.) is one to cultivate as Christian girls.

The characteristic of meekness is quite often misunderstood. Meek is not a synonym for stupid, weak, door-mat or insipid. Meek represents a young horse broken to harness, which has no less energy or strength, but can be controlled to pull heavy loads consistently.

James gives a fine illustration on the subject of horses and bridles in relation to the tongue. "Now if we put the horses bridles into their mouths that they may obey us, we turn about their whole body also." (James 3:3.) In verse five: "So the tongue also is a little member, and boasteth great things. Behold, how much wood is kindled by how small a fire!" Verse seven says: "For every kind of beasts and birds, of creeping things and things in the sea, is tamed, and hath been tamed by mankind: but the tongue can no man tame; it is a restless evil, it is full of deadly poison." (James 3:7.)

So, what can one do about controlling the tongue, if it is impossible to tame it? Sure we have seen trained tigers, lions and elephants in the circus. We have watched dolphins and seals perform on television as well as parakeets. No doubt a flea circus has had our attention at some time.

Does the Bible tell us to let our tongues wag because we can do nothing about it? No! A thousand times no! The teaching in the book of James is that one person can not tame the tongue of another person, but one can bridle one's own tongue. It may be a difficult task, but the Christian is to control the members of his own body. (Colossians 3:5—11; Romans 6:12, 13.) Self control is one of the Christian graces. (2 Peter 1:5—8.) Self control is also listed in Galatians 5:22, 23 as fruit of the Spirit.

Serious illness may result from a hemorrhage of the mouth, physically, even death may be the result if it is not stopped. Likewise, a flow of evil speaking from the mouth may cause spiritual weakness or even spiritual death. "Life and death are in the power of the tongue." (Proverbs 18:21.)

Hearts And Flowers

The month of February has a special significance for Americans, because we celebrate the birthdays of two of our favorite former presidents, Washington and Lincoln. A cherry tree and a hatchet and a log cabin are symbols that remind us of historic events. February 14 is a date in which most girls are interested, it is Valentine day.Symbols are cupid, his bow and arrow, as well as hearts and flowers.

When I was growing up (way back when) we looked forward with pleasure to the party at school, when the Valentine box was opened and the beautiful hearts were distributed. There were comic valentines for laughs and many romantic messages, such as: "Be my Valentine" and "I love you." We had fun for weeks with construction paper, scissors, paste and lace paper doileys. Some startling creations appeared! Rarely if ever, did a store bought heart get into our party. In some schools there was the crowning of the Valentine Queen, the most popular girl in school. Along with the fun, we were taught at home and at school to remember the lonely and sick with our hearts and flowers — to share our happiness.

Since it is impossible for me to think of February 14 without hearts and flowers, I want to feature roses, probably the best loved of all flowers.

"The perfume of the gods," according to the Greeks, was just another way of saying roses. The history of cultivated roses begins in antiquity. They have been found in the dry bouquets taken from Egyptian tombs; they are mentioned in the oldest known writings; the Chinese have grown them for countless centuries.

There are preserved specimens of the Damask rose found in the Pompeian excavations. There are imprints of roses on coins on the Island of Rhodes, so named because of the extensive culture and trade in roses.

Mohammedan invasions of Syria, India and lands bordering the Mediterranean, resulted in the distribution of locally known roses to Spain. The Roman invaders of northern Europe and England, brought to these lands the roses of the Mediterranean region.

Evidently rose water and fresh or dried rose petals were used by the early races of Asia, as well as by the Greeks and Romans. The essential oil contained in roses is reputed to have been discovered accidently in ancient Persia. It takes about 3000 pounds of petals to produce 1 pound of rose oil.

Would a rose smell just as sweet if it were called by another name? It is perhaps surprising to learn that in the rose family are apples, pears, quince, plum, peach, cherry, raspberry, blackberry, strawberry and spirea. The genus rosa includes 100 or more species, and there are native roses in every national division as well as in every geologic and geographic division of the northern hemisphere. The word rose is even used for plants not at all related to roses, suh as Christmas rose, rose of Sharon and rock rose. So much from my bouquet of roses to the column readers.

May I suggest that you read the story of Mary of Bethany as recorded in Matthew 26:6—13; Mark 14:3—9; John 12: 1—8. Mary used the very expensive ointment on Jesus, her Lord, to show her love. Some of the disciples criticized her, but Jesus said: "Let her alone . . . She hath done what she could, she hath anointed my body beforehand for the burying." In about a week the body of Jesus would be in the tomb, and friends would be carrying sweet spices, perfume and ointment for that very purpose, as was the custom of that day. In our times, we send flowers to the graves of our loved ones. Mary's anointing was equal to giving flowers to the living. How often do we hear: "I had rather have my flowers now than after I am dead"? Therefore, girls, think of giving flowers to the living, in a thoughtful deed or a kind word. You will be dispensing the most precious perfume in all the world and you, yourself, will "smell as sweet as a rose."

Topics For Discussion:

1. Bible's most honored woman.
2. Paul's evaluation of Timothy.
3. Influence of Lois and Eunice.
4. Jesus' concern for his mother as he hung on the cross.
5. Sentiment of "Heart Portraits."
6. "The foolish woman is clamorous; she is simple and knoweth nothing."
7. Why it is good to be quiet and busy.
8. True meaning of meek.
9. Teaching of James on taming and bridling tongues.
10. "Life and death are in the power of the tongue."
11. Interesting facts about "the perfume of the gods."
12. Mary of Bethany and the expensive ointment she lavished on her Lord.
13. The best time to give our flowers.

CHAPTER XI

Love That Tree!

"He is the possessor of dull eyes or a flinty soul who does not feel a thrill when in the presence of a beautiful tree. This friendship with trees is age old and is one of man's finest experiences." — *H.E. Jaques* professor of Biology, Iowa Wesleyan College.

Daily we read in current magazines or newspapers, about conservation and the need of protecting our environment. We must be reminded of the importance of this matter. In ancient times there were laws about cutting trees (Deuteronomy 20:19, 20) and protecting bird's nests with their young. (Deuteronomy 22:6, 7.) This is not only an interesting fact, but shows God's wisdom in instructing his people.

Please share with me the following clipping from Roadside Bulletin.

TO THE WAYFARER

(poem fastened to trees in the Portugese forest.)

Ye who pass by and would raise your hand against me hearken ere you harm me.

I am the heat of your hearth on the cold winter nights, the friendly shade screening you from summer sun, and my fruits are refreshing draughts, quenching your thirst as you journey on.

I am the beam that holds your house, the board of your table, the bed on which you lie, the timber that builds your boat.

I am the handle of you hoe, the door of your homestead, the wood of your cradle, and the shell of your coffin.

I am the bread of kindness and the flower of beauty.

Ye who pass by, listen to my prayer: HARM ME NOT!

From the Florence Times — Tri Cities Daily last year in the section Life Scene, I clipped: THE TREE SPEAKS:

"I am an indispensable part of man's life. I am the paper that feeds the press and brings you the news each morning from the ends of the earth. I make books wherein are written your laws and constitutions, your memory of history and your knowledge of science, and I bind the sacred pages of your Bibles.

"I have served for bridles, boats, fences, wagons, charcoal, gunpowder, tool handles, telegraph poles, gun stocks, pipe bowls, baskets, barrels, boxes and mosaics. I can be a match stem or a ship mast, a rolling pin or a roof beam, a doorstep or a sanctuary. Wood is the spindle and shuttle of the weaver, the scaffold of the mason, the form of the cement worker, the plow handle of the farmer, and the whole trade of the carpenter.

"I am clothes to a man to shield his body, and an ornament to woman to reveal her grace. I furnish the humblest cabin and finish the most glorious cathedral. I was the cedar of Lebanon, the olive of Gethsemane, the groves of Gilead, and the myrtle of all pleasant gardens. I was the ark of Noah, the Santa Maria of Columbus, the Armada of Spain and the fleet of Nelson.

"Your rivers are fed from springs and streams are kept clean and cool in my forest depths, and they lend their power to your mills by virtue of my service. Without me mountain, hill and stream will return to their primal emptiness.

"I have made your gardens fair with shade and bloom. I have sheltered you and warmed you. I have ministered to your need from your first father to this hour, and I have served you from your cradle to your grave. I was the wood of the altar where you worshipped God, and the incense that ascended with your prayers. I was the rod of Aaron, the ark of the Covenant, the bush that burned with the glory of Jehovah, and the cedar of the Temple. I was the substance that took the tool marks of the Carpenter's Son, the crown of thorns they pressed on his head, and the cross whereon they slew him at last.

"And yet you Have not loved me, nor remembered all my mercies. I have taken the brunt of your savage ignorance; I have carried the scars of your dawning civilization; and suffered the wreckage of your modern power. I have known the fire of your wanton carelessness, the torture of your senseless progress, and the betrayal of your Judas' bargaining for a little gain. But I continue my service gently and humbly to the end. I can do no other. I am the gift of God! I am the friend of man!"

Young women, I urge you to consider thoughtfully this Conservation Pledge: I GIVE MY PLEDGE AS AN AMERICAN TO SAVE AND FAITHFULLY TO DEFEND FROM WASTE THE NATURAL RESOURCES OF MY COUNTY; ITS SOIL AND MINERALS; ITS FORESTS, WATERS AND WILDLIFE.

Anchor Of the Soul

According to Greek mythology, the first woman in the world was Pandora. She was given a box by the Creator and told to guard it well but never open it. The myth relates how Pandora's curiosity overpowered her caution and she opened the box just enough to peep in. Out came all the diseases and troubles that have plagued the human race through the ages. Pandora wept bitterly and regretted her disobedience. Later she heard a soft voice calling from the box: "Let me out, please. I can help you." She was astonished and replied, "No, I have done enough harm." But the voice continued to plead with Pandora, "Let me out!" Pandora asked, "Who are you?" The answer came from the box, "My name is Hope, and you need me now with all the troubles in the world. If you release me, I can make the world a better place to live in." So Pandora opened the box and Hope came out, according to the myth.

Hope is a big word in our vocabulary, but perhaps we use the word incorrectly. Many times we are just wishing when we say we are hoping. For instance young girls may say that they hope: for a beautiful face and a shapely figure; to lose ten pounds weight without going on a strict diet; to win the attention of the handsomest boy in school; to have a date for the football banquet; to make the honor roll; to win a scholarship to college; to have her weekly allowance doubled! et cetera. That is just plain wishing. Let us notice the difference.

Hope is always composed of two elements: desire and expectation. As an illustration, one would not say, "I hope to have the measles soon, since I was exposed to the disease." One might expect to have the measles, but certainly would not have a desire to be sick. I could not tell my friends that I hope to travel around the world next summer. Although I may have the desire for such a trip, I do not expect to have

77

an opportunity to travel.

Suppose one of your friends went to the doctor for a check up and cancer was discovered. The first reaction is despair. But the doctor says surgery will remove the malignancy and then the friend has hope, because of his desire to live and the expectation that an operation gives. Many patients recover from serious illnesses because they have the will to get well, with the expectation. Hope is a powerful motivation.

In Ecclesiastes 9:4 we read, "For to him that is joined with all the living, there is hope; for a living dog is better than a dead lion." This passage must be the source of the quotation we often hear: "Where there is life, there is hope." Life is precious. The most humble and lowly creature that is alive is of more value than a kingly or royal subject that is dead.

We learn not to give up; to keep struggling. Sometimes we get discouraged in our efforts when we do not at first succeed. Let us be glad that we are alive, with health and ambition. This attitude will help at school when examination time comes. We study for examinations. We hope to pass because there is a desire to make good grades plus hard work. No use to hope for passing grades without study!

Hope is called the anchor of the soul in Hebrews 6:18, 19 which is both "sure and steadfast." An anchor is a thing which steadies another thing; as the anchor of a suspension bridge. A boat needs an anchor, when cast overboard it hooks on the bottom of the body of water and holds the boat in place. In this life, trials and troubles can be endured and overcome because of hope. From serious financial problems to lovers' quarrels, in every area of life, we learn to "hang in there" hoping for a better tomorrow.

Every Christian has a hope of heaven. He not only desires to live eternally with God but expects to enjoy this blessing because he has obeyed his Lord's commands. (Hebrews 5:9; Matthew 7:21.) In case a non-Christian is reading this article and would like to know how to inherit eternal life, just follow these simple directions. To know God is eternal life. (John 17:3.) To know him is to believe in him. (Hebrews 11:6.) It is impossible to know of the great Creator, his love, mercy and long suffering without loving him. (John 3:16.) To love him is to keep his commandments. (John 14:15; 1 John 2:3, 4.) To keep his commandments is eternal life. (Titus 1:2; 3:7.) Love is the foundation principle of Christianity. We learn to know God and Christ, his Son, from the Bible, the word of God. (Romans 10:17.) Believers were told to repent and be baptized. (Acts 2:38.) Believers make the good confession. (Matthew 16:16; Romans 6:4.) They are raised to walk in newness of life as Christians. "For in hope were we saved; but hope that is seen is not hope; for who hopeth for that which he seeth? But if we hope for that which we see not then do we with patience wait for it." (Romans 8:24, 25.)

The following was copied from an old book of sermons by the pioneer preachers:

Faith destroys love of sin.
Repentance destroys the practice of sin.
Baptism puts one in a saved state, where one has hope of salvation.

Faith connects us with God.
Hope connects us with heaven.
Love makes us like God and fits us for heaven.

Faith is present.
Hope is future.
Love is for all time — eternal.

A Junior Miss, Missionary

Alicejoy Kee, daughter of Mr. and Mrs. Windle Kee, Kumba, Cameroun, West Africa, is featured this month in our column. A young girl with ambition, courage and dedication should be an inspiration to all of us who read of her accomplishments.

"I thought one had to be old to serve as a missionary," said one girl in a class discussion. "I thought that one must preach the gospel to be called a missionary," said another girl. A third girl spoke, "Preachers' wives are called missionaries because they help teach and serve in many ways." The discussion continued with this comment, "Preachers' children are helpers too, both boys and girls."

The class teacher responded, "Yes, it is true that every member of a missionary family, old enough to be responsible, assumes certain duties, because they are so trained. However, only the men are public preachers of the gospel. Let's think of the meaning of the word missionary – of or belonging to missions, especially religious missions. A commission is an order or instruction authorizing a person to perform a duty. Jesus gave such instructions to his apostles just before his ascension, which is called the Great Commission, recorded in Matthew 28:18–20; Mark 16:15, 16; Luke 24:44–49. We think of the words: Go into all the world and preach the gospel, as our marching orders for Christians in the 20th century. When individuals or families are sent on such a mission to any part of the world, they are called missionaries."

The girls then wanted the teacher to tell them what young girls could do in a place like Africa. Here is the story.

Alicejoy started working in the Christian Mobile Clinic as a "dresser," cleaning and bandaging tropical ulcers and abscesses, and then began dispensing medicines. One of her duties was taking temperatures and blood pressures (sometimes 100 in a day.) Perhaps her worst patient was a man who had wrecked his motorcycle. It took her forty five minutes to "clean up" his wounds so the doctor could treat him.

An automobile wreck really tested Alicejoy's ability to cope with emergencies. She rescued her seventeen year old cousin from the vehicle, pulled off her slip and used it to help stop the bleeding, for bandages, remaining calm, giving assurance to others.

When Miss Kee stopped working full time for the mobile clinic, she volunteered to make the calamine lotion, the cough syrup, diarrhea medicine and liquid aspirin in large amounts for the clinic.

One day while working in the clinic building, which had a thatched roof, Alicejoy looked up to see a six foot snake hanging from the ceiling. What would you do under such circumstances? Would most girls stay cool, calm and collected? Alicejoy had learned how to cope when such happenings occurred. Never did she throw up her hands, scream and run! Many times these huge snakes appeared in the clinic building.

In addition to her medical work, Alicejoy taught children's Bible classes. For a year, she taught the children of the missionaries, often giving parties for them. She also taught native women (who could read a little) how to do the Bible Correspondence course.

Miss Kee also had time to complete two of the courses at the Cameroun Christian Bible School for college credit and conducted home studies in connection with this. Her studious habits and teaching ability were recognized by all the church leaders. When a Ladies' Lectureship was planned, she was on the program as one of the main lecturers, because she had a message of inspiration. It was a great occasion for the female population, both Christian and non-Christian, who came from distant villages to be instructed about Christ and his church.

Sewing was a skill which this talented miss cultivated. Perhaps her mother helped and encouraged her. She did not have an electric machine, but an old fashioned treadle sewing machine. In the native markets there were beautiful materials, so Alicejoy (in her spare time) made a wardrobe for herself.

Alicejoy was just sixteen years old when she went for the second tour in Africa, so it was necessary to complete her high school work, which had to be done by correspondence. During this eighteen month time, she worked hard on her studies, receiving her high school diploma in March 1976 with straight A's. Most young girls dream of graduation day, with all of its pomp and ceremony, gala parties, receiving presents from admiring friends and relatives.

The graduation party for Alicejoy Kee was different to say the least, one she will never forget. Her mother made her a cap and gown which looked great. Thirty five of her black friends came to help her celebrate. Soon afterward she left Africa to come back to the United States. These African friends sang three farewell songs, written especially for the occasion.

This summer, Alicejoy is working in a hospital as a nurse's aid. She plans to enter Oklahoma Christian College this fall, to major in nursing. Then she will rejoin her family in Africa as a full time missionary.

An Autumnal Allegory

A drive into the country side at this season of the year can be an exhilarating experience, because of the beauty of the trees. There they stand in gorgeous array! From a distance the hillsides appear as a rare tapestry, patterns of dark and lighter greens of evergreens interwoven with the bright reds, golds and browns of the deciduous trees. Turn around a curve suddenly and there appears a tree at least fifty feet high of solid gold, truly a breath taking sight. Myriads of scarlet sumac line the roadside. In the background, hickory, maple, oak, with black gum and sweet gum, sycamore and countless other trees and shrubs all have a distinctive color. Nature lovers stand in awe and quote lines from the famous poem by Joyce Kilmer:

> "I think that I shall never see
> A poem lovely as a tree . . .
> Poems are made by fools like me,
> But only God can make a tree."

After a long, cold winter, Spring is most welcome, with the new leaves, tender shoots of plants and colorful flowers. We praise God for the new life of another year. In autumn, however, the grains, fruits and flowers have reached maturity, the height of perfection, the very peak of loveliness. There is a grandeur about the autumn, a deeper richer beauty, which the spring does not possess. The harvest is more important than the beginning of growth in the vegetable kingdom. The wind comes by and the gaudy leaves flutter to the earth, brown, red, yellow and even a green one occasionally. A feeling of mixed emotions comes over us as we watch the falling leaves and see their little lives expire. Such a spectacle suggests the following analogy.

The woodland is the world; the leaves are the people who live here; the wind is death. We are like the leaves

83

which live for a season, fluttering cheerfully or moving restlessly, on the sturdy trees, seemingly secure, only to be torn away unexpectedly.

The green leaves resemble lives cut off before life has run its course. We despair to see the freshness and happiness of youth cease. Perhaps we are reminded to make the most of every day; use every opportunity presented to us; be diligent; be useful. A short life surcharged with endeavor is worth more than a long life of listless existence.

Red leaves stand for that hilarious group, the pleasure seekers, who lead a frivolous, thoughtless life. They are always rushing here and there, seeking excitement. They do not stop to question where this course will lead them. "The god of this world hath blinded their eyes." (2 Corinthians 4:4.)

They are deaf to the voice of conscience. They are not ready to be snatched into eternity, but like the leaves, when the wind comes to tear them from the trees, they have no power to resist. The merry, carefree life may be pleasant for a season, but lends no hope for a future life of peace and joy beyond the grave.

There is a likeness in the yellow leaves to the golden lives of noble Christian characters. They are by nature lovely, delighting all that know their beauty of spirit. Golden lives are truly a blessing to the world. "Even so let you light shine before men; that they may see your good works and glorify your Father who is in heaven." (Matthew 5:16.)

Think of brown leaves as lukewarm, uncommitted Christians, with just enough religion to make them miserable. They are not scarlet, immoral people, but live drab, do nothing, fearful-of-criticism, weak, wishy-washy lives, instead of beautiful, golden, self-sacrificing, busy, useful lives of dedicated Christians, who have the hope of eternal life. (Titus 3:7; Romans 6:23; 1 John 1:17.)

In this tapestry of life, what is your color scheme? How are you weaving, young people?

Topics For Discussion:

1. God's laws in the Old Testament to protect trees and bird nests.
2. Poem fastened to trees in Portugese forest.
3. Comment on "The Tree Speaks".
4. Protecting our environemnt in America.
5. Pandora in Greek Mythology.
6. Difference in wishing and hoping.
7. Illustration of desire and expectation as elements of hope.
8. How hope is the anchor of the soul.
9. How to inherit eternal life.
10. Notes from pioneer book of sermons.
11. What is a missionary.
12. Alicejoy's work in an African clinic.
13. Alicejoy's ability to stay calm in emergencies.
14. Alicejoy's part in the teaching program of the mission; her sewing skill; high school graduation.
15. The meaning of each leaf color in Autumnal Allegory.
16. Which color represents you in the tapestry of life.

CHAPTER XII

Friendship

"The language of friendship is not words, but meanings. It is an intelligence above language." — *Thoreau*.

LESSON AT LUNCH

Two girls were preparing a picnic lunch. The cookies had been baked, the potato salad made and next they had to make sandwiches. "You slice the boiled ham", said Mary; "while I spread the mayonnaise on the bread." "O.K." replied Alice, "where will I find the butcher knife?" Alice found the knife but complained, "This knife is not sharp enough to cut the ham, What shall I do now?" Mary said, "Just wait a minute and I will get the knife sharpener and I'll whet this knife to a keen edge."

As Alice watched the demonstration, she said: "That reminds me of our Bible lesson yesterday." Mary laughed, "What do you mean? How on earth could this job make you think of the Bible?" Alice picked up a Bible and opened the book, reading from Proverbs 27:17: "Iron sharpeneth iron; So a man sharpeneth the countenance of his friend."

Alice continued, "Our teacher explained that as hard iron or steel will bring a knife to a better edge when it is properly whetted against it; so one friend may be the means of exciting another to reflect, think . . . "

Mary listened, then replied, "Now, I get it — a person in conversation with a friend, promotes intelligent thinking, which shows in the face. The expression on one's face tells the world how that person feels — happiness, grief, anger or boredom."

Alice continued, "You know how we get excited and enthused when we talk to our friends about their experience in winning souls in the West Indies. Such conversations caused us to determine to be soul winners too."

Mary held up a very sharp knife and said, "This is a good illustration. Perhaps we can try harder to get more of our friends interested in using their vacations next summer to go on a campaign for Christ."

Alice continued, "Our teacher quoted from a man named Scott: 'Friends of like dispositions whet each other's ingenuity; suggest useful hints and good counsels and encourage one another. Indeed it has been observed, that the most useful inventions have originated from the collision of men's thoughts, when earnestly engaged in conversation.' "

As the girls finished the sandwich making, they commented on what a good lesson they had learned from a common kitchen knife, about friendship.

The Value Of Friends

A college professor was lecturing on geography. He explained to the class the great expanse and the vast territory of the State of Texas. One of the students asked him: "Professor, do you think that the whole population of the United States could be put into the State of Texas?" The professor thought for a moment. Then he said: "Yes, if they were all friends." That really is the world's problem today. How can we live together on this crowded earth, so many billions of us, unless we are friends?

Jesus emphasized that we must live by love. He invited people to help to build the beloved community, the kingdom of friends, based on love. "Friendship is the only thing in the world concerning the usefulness of which all mankind are agreed." — *Cicero*.

Said Mrs. Browning, the poet, to Charles Kingsley, the novelist, "What is the secret of your life? Tell me, that I may make mine beautiful also." Thinking a moment, the beloved old author replied, "I had a friend."

It has also been said: "Friendship is the highest degree of perfection in society." — *Montaigne*.

From the Bible we read of the wonderful friendship of David and Jonathan. (1 Sam. 18:1; 2 Sam. 1:26.) It is recorded that Abraham was the friend of God. (James 2:23.) What an honor! We also read: "And Jehovah spake unto Moses face to face, as a man speaketh unto his friend." (Ex. 33:11.) Jesus called his disciples friends. (John 15:14.)

Consider the true meaning of Proverbs 27:19: "As in water face answereth to face, so the heart of man to man." In clear water we see our reflection, as in a mirror. Likewise, kindred spirits communicate face to face and heart to heart. Our innermost thoughts, desires, ambitions and even sorrows are reflected in the pool of friendship.

Like Tapestry

Girls, our lives are somewhat like a tapestry, which we weave day by day, as long as we live. Some of the threads are dark and some are bright. It takes the contrast to make beautiful the whole. Life is made up of lights and shadows. Sometimes the tapestry will be full of flaws, but mostly the weaving is smooth. God has furnished the pattern to go by, but every person weaves with the material at hand, in a very personal, individual way and each person has an entirely different design. My tapestry has some very bright and beautiful threads of friendship, which have enriched my life.

REMINISCENCE

In the fall of 1919, I was eighteen years old, excited and happy about going to college. My destination was David Lipscomb College, Nashville, Tenn. I rode the train all the way from south Alabama, arriving many hours later at the old L and N Station. A figure of Mercury, with winged feet, on top of the building, which was a land mark then, intrigued me greatly. The last part of the journey was made from Church Street on the Glendale street car. Then a long walk up Caldwell Lane to the school campus.

Avalon Home was the name of the girls' dormitory. I shall never forget the huge trees, blue grass and rock fences, a beautiful location with a view of Granny White Hills in the distance. This was to be my home for the next two years and I loved it.

After a brief look at the administration building, Harding Hall, and Lindsay Hall, the boys' dormitory, and Aunt Mag Lipscomb's house (the entire campus) I was ready to be assigned a room by sister Boles, the Matron.

One of the first girls to welcome me was Ruth, who asked me to be her room mate and to join the Kappa Nu Literary Society. Two other girls shared our room. There were some real adjustments to make. An only child, I was used to rooming alone, with a quiet time to study and plenty of closet space for my clothes. Sometimes I was frustrated, but most of the time, I enjoyed the companionship of new friends.

My parents had taught me to be careful in a choice of friends. In a new environment especially, they said, one is judged by the company one keeps.

"True happiness consists not in the multitude of friends, but in the worth and choice." — *Jonson.* That was my guide, in making friends. Perhaps that is the reason these friendships have endured for over half a century!

The following quotation comes to mind: "Friendship's the image of eternity, in which there is nothing moveable." — *Lilly.*

SALT OF THE EARTH

New friends I cherish and treasure their worth
But old friends to me are the salt of the earth.
Friends are like garments that everyone wears
New ones are needed for dress-up affairs;
But when we're at leisure, we're more apt to choose
The clothes that we purchased with last season's shoes.

Things we grow used to are things we love best
The ones we are certain have weathered the test.
And isn't it true, since we're talking of friends,
That new ones bring pleasure when everything blends?
But when we want someone who thinks as we do,
And who fits, as I said, like last summer's shoe,
We turn to friends who have stuck through the years,
Who echo our laughter and dry up our tears:
They know every weakness and fault we possess,
But somehow forget them in friendship's caress.

The story is old, yet fragrant and sweet;
I've said it before, but just let me repeat;
New friends I cherish and treasure their worth,
But old friends to me are the salt of the earth.

— Author Unknown

Morning Devotions

Do you have a morning glory vine blooming at your house?
You don't? I am sorry that you are missing such a lovely
spectacle during a two or three month period. I have two
trellises on an east porch covered with Heavenly Blue blossoms. Here I can go for private devotions early in the morning: gaze, receive inspiration for the day, thank God for such
beauty, not forgetting to express gratitude for all my other
blessings.

Recently, during a morning meditation, a happening in
Alabama was uppermost in my mind. I began to compare it
with Luke 10:30—37. I am sure you recognize the Bible cita-
tion as the famous Good Samaritan story.

A series of tornados struck in Alabama, April 30, 1974,
leaving miles of devastation in Madison, Limestone, Morgan
and Lawrence counties. There were many deaths, hundreds
of injuries to people and animals as well as millions of dollars
in damages to homes, farms and businesses. Many of the
people who were left safe in their homes were in shock.
Robert England was not in the path of the tornado. His
family and property were secure, but when he began to view
the plight of his neighbors, he felt compelled to do something.
His wife, Mary, agreed. Her question was, "How?" Robert
replied, "We will find a way." After a long discussion and
prayer, they came to a decision. Robert went to the bank
and borrowed money. Then he asked his boss for three
weeks leave of absence. Now, he literally rolled up his sleeves
ready to go to work, because he had made plans.

Some neighbors without shelter were Mennonites. The
Englands took fourteen men, women and children into their
home for lodging. The next week the number grew to
twenty three accepting their hospitality. Permission was
obtained to use the church building for a first aid center,

where victims could rest and wait for a permanent place to stay. A friend, who was an invalid, confined to her bed, volunteered to use the telephone to relay messages. So the colossal task began of turning chaos into order after a tornado.

Robert and his crew of Mennonite men got tools and went about repairing, rebuilding and cleaning up debris. The women helped Mary prepare meals along with other household tasks. The noon meal was carried to the men on the job to save time. Supper and breakfast were served at home. Here is a sample breakfast menu: Six pounds bacon, two pounds sausage, four loaves of bread or six big pans of biscuits, juice and coffee. Individuals, and some organizations sent donations of food and money to help during the three weeks. Mary used her ingenuity in making ends meet, preparing wholesome and nourishing food. One other woman was a faithful helper besides the Mennonites.

When bath time came, transportation was furnished to the National Guard Armory, where their facilities were used. Also permission was granted to use showers at the Morgan County High School.

At night after supper, the group was not too tired to engage in a little fun and games. A thirteen year old boy brought his banjo and provided music. Sometimes everyone played games, while at other times they read and studied the Bible.

News of the disaster in Alabama was on T.V. and radio. As a result, hundreds of volunteers came from other states to help. They were welcomed by the Red Cross, State and County officials. The work was coordinated in a fine way for the benefit of all.

Let us compare this happening in Alabama with the

Bible story in Luke 10:30—37. (1) The tornado was like the robbers who stripped the Mennonites (of another faith) of their possessions, leaving them half dead. (2) The priest and Levite who saw and passed by on the other side were like persons in the area who saw but went on their way to a regular job or to work in their own fields. (3) Robert England, like the Good Samaritan, when he saw was moved with compassion. He took as many persons into his house as he could shelter, doing what he could to pour on oil and wine, render first aid and relieve suffering. (4) The Good Samaritan gave money to the innkeeper saying: "Whatsoever thou spendeth more I when I come back will repay thee." Robert England not only used his own funds freely, but also gave his time and energy.

Robert and Mary England showed their faith by their works. (James 2:14—17.) Also they proved their love for God. (1 John 3:17.) Our attitude toward our fellowmen shows that we love God according to Matthew 25:40. This is an illustration of practical Christianity. As a direct result of the effort of the Englands, two families were converted to Christ. In addition, Robert and his crew, built, renovated or restored forty eight houses, so families could be reunited and go back to normal living. Lasting friendships were made and there was the joy of serving others. Of course building supplies were donated by private citizens and organizations. Licensed electricians and plumbers gave time and labor.

Jesus related the story of Luke 10:30—37 in answer to the question: "Who is my neighbor?" (Luke 10:29.) At the conclusion of the story, Jesus asked, "Which of these three (priest, Levite, Good Samaritan) thinkest thou proved neighbor unto him that fell among robbers?" The answer was, "He that showed mercy." Jesus replied, "GO AND DO THOU LIKEWISE." These words apply to us today.

One Day At A Time

How much wiser and happier we all would be if we simply would take things as they come to us from day to day.

Montaigne wrote in one of his essays: "I love rainy and dirty weather as ducks do. The change either of air or climate doth nothing distemper me." He took life as it came to him and found no fault. He blamed most of his misfortunes upon his own unwise acts.

The evil behind all fear is being fearful. Worry has never changed an event in all the history of time. Most of the things worried about never happen anyway. We need to be calmly armed against all occurrences, but not with fear or worry. Contrariwise, with courage and a high heart!

It has been said that the "good die young." But so do the bad die young! Also it is true that the good and bad both live to ripe old age. Life is like that. Depressions come, but they pass. They always have. The informed take things as they come because they have a backward and forward vision.

We know that we are traveling down a road. We know that we shall meet difficulties: streams to ford, hills to climb, apparently impossible situations to meet, and sometimes we are bound to lose our way. Darkness will hover about us. We can only take things as they come and travel on – guided by our unfaltering purpose and our abiding faith.

We are not in a contest with Fate. We are all children of destiny — and "it doth not appear what we shall be" nor what our end may be. We can only as Stevenson has written, "travel hopefully."

"Let no youth have an anxiety about the upshot of his

education whatever the line may be," wrote William James in his great essay on Habit. "If he keeps faithfully busy each hour of the working day, he may safely leave the final result to itself. He can with perfect certainty count on waking up some fine morning, to find himself one of the competent ones of his generation.

"By taking things as they come and doing our best to make them come right, we can face the future with confidence and happy hope." (*George Matthew Adams*)

Thanksgiving

One day in the year has been set aside as a national holiday, for the express purpose of giving thanks to God for all of our blessings. This we must do with hearts full of gratitude. Our blessings are almost too numerous to count, but this Thanksgiving I want to thank God for the privilege of knowing a very great Christian woman, sister Sarah Andrews, a missionary to Japan for many years. Her life has been an inspiration to me through the years, because of her unselfish service in a foreign land.

Sister Sarah's greatest work was teaching women and girls about Jesus. She produced literature in the Japanese language for her classes, translating much of the Bible also.

This woman of God's philosophy of life was based on Phillipians 4:6, 7: "In nothing be anxious; but in everything by prayer and supplication with thanksgiving let your requests be made known unto God. And the peace of God, which passeth all understanding, shall guard your hearts and your thoughts in Christ Jesus."

Sarah Andrews summed up her way of life like this: ANXIOUS FOR NOTHING, THANKFUL FOR ANYTHING, PRAYERFUL ABOUT EVERYTHING. She was not anxious and fretful about material things, but lived very simply, like her Japanese neighbors, as she taught them the "unsearchable riches". She was indeed thankful for anything and prayerful about everything in her life.

During World War II, our planes were bombing Japan, but sister Andrews was not jittery and worried about her safety. She said that it was as near heaven from Japan as from America. One night the village she lived in was bombed. Her little house was left standing in the midst of ruins. People were amazed at her courage and serenity. She firmly believed: "When you have accomplished your daily task, go to sleep in peace; God is awake." — *Victor Hugo*.

Let's thank God for such an example of faith and pray that our faith may grow.

Topics For Discussion:

1. Thoreau's definition of the language of friendship.
2. Lesson from a kitchen knife.
3. Quotation from Cicero.
4. Friends in the Bible.
5. Guide in making friends.
6. "The Salt Of The Earth."
7. Compare the tornado in Alabama to The Good Samaritan story in four ways.
8. Results of good deeds by one family who acted as good neighbors.
9. Why worry never helps.
10. How to "Travel hopefully" day by day.

11. The philosophy of life of Sis. Sarah Andrews, missionary to Japan.
12. Story from World War II.

CHAPTER XIII

Whom Shall We Invite To Dinner?

Mary and Alice were planning a formal dinner party during the holdiay season. They were inviting a very select group of girls and their boy friends. The guest list included the most prominent students in high school: president of the student body, captain of the football team, most of the players, all of the cheerleaders, the beauty queen, and all of her court. The decorations were fabulous.

A group of musicians from the city were invited to furnish entertainment. They were exchanging gifts with expensive price tags. The two girls were excited about the beautiful new dresses just bought for the occasion.

As they discussed last minute details and lettered the place cards, Mary said: "I am glad we got the best catering service in town." Alice replied: "No one can top this party, that's for sure! However, we have been too extravagant and spent too much money on it. Maybe we should have had a more simple affair." Mary stared at her in unbelief and asked, "Have you changed your mind about our plans?" Alice answered: "Well, I have been giving it some thought, in fact I am not so sure we should have this party." "Why not?" Mary asked.

"In Bible class Sunday morning, we had a lesson that put doubts in my mind. Listen to this reading," Alice said, as she reached for her Bible and opened it at Luke 14:12—14: "When thou makest a dinner or supper, call not thy friends, nor thy brethren, nor thy kinsmen, nor thy rich neighbors; lest haply they also bid thee again, and a recompense be made thee. But when thou makest a feast, bid the poor, the maimed, the lame, the blind; and thou shalt be blessed; because they have not wherewith to recompense thee: for thou shalt be recompensed in the resurrection of the just."

"Who said that?" Mary wanted to know. "It was Jesus", Alice replied. "Do you mean that Jesus said not to invite our friends and family to dinner? Why not, please tell me!" asked a disturbed girl.

Alice continued, "Our Sunday School teacher explained it this way. Jesus was invited to eat at the house of a Pharisee. He noticed as the guests came in how they took the best seats. They did not have chairs at the tables as we have, but reclined on couches. The chief seats or most important positions at an entertainment among them, as well as among the Romans, was the middle part of the middle couch, each couch holding three.

"At a banquet in our country, we think of the speakers' table as the chief seats, where the master of ceremonies, and guest speakers are always placed. We know better than to set ourselves there without an invitation! It would be very embarrassing to be asked to move! Jesus' teaching to these guests was: 'For everyone that exalteth himself shall be humbled; and he that humbleth himself shall be exalted.'

"Then Jesus talked to the persons who in a selfish way invite others to a feast," continued Alice. "Friends, family and rich neighbors will likely have their host for dinner. Jesus does not mean that we should never have our best friends to eat with us, but it is far better to plan to relieve the poor and distressed than to give a dinner for those who do not need it and expect to be entertained in return. Of course we can eat with relatives and friends, but not only with them. The Christian has compassion for the needy and is interested in providing for the less fortunate, rather than merely satisfying a selfish pride in entertaining those who do not need it."

"That makes sense to me," said Mary, "perhaps I never read Luke 14:12—14 with understanding. Let's cancel this dinner party. While you were talking, I read verse 13 again: 'But when thou makest a feast, bid the poor, the maimed, the lame, the blind: and thou shalt be blessed; because they have not wherewith to recompense thee.' "

As a result of this decision by Mary and Alice, who were not really selfish, just thoughtless, many persons were made happy. Patients at The Crippled Children's Hospital had a gala holiday; lonely senior citizens at a nursing home were remembered with a musical program; students at the blind school were taken on a trip and served refreshments.

Giving And Getting

During the holiday season, we all have our minds on giving and getting. Quite often getting is given top priority. Just what is the proper attitude for the Christian? The following passage of scripture will help us decide.

In Acts 20:35 we read that Paul said: "In all things I gave you an example, that so laboring ye ought to help the weak, and to remember the words of the Lord Jesus, that he himself said, it is more blessed to give than to receive." This was from a farewell speech to the elders of the church at Ephesus. Paul reminds them that he not only preached to them for three years, but set an example of working with his own hands to support himself and those with him. He had not accumulated money to hoard, or spend for selfish purposes. He was interested in the souls of the people and not their possessions.

Sure, the preacher had to have food, shelter and clothing,

the necessities of life. He was willing to work for his living and preach the gospel too. In addition to supplying himself and his helpers with these necessary things, Paul worked to help the weak (the poor, sick, feeble, crippled and infirm.) This class of people could not help themselves, but were dependent on the generosity of others. Paul was willing to sacrifice his own comfort and pleasure to serve others because he had the spirit of Christ. He could quote the words of his Lord to the brethren at Ephesus because it was his way of life. "It is more blessed to give than to receive" can serve as a timely reminder to us.

Since the word blessed can be translated happy, young people may wonder why it is possible to be happier in giving than receiving. Most of us think that we are content to be on the receiving end of the line.

Truly it is more blessed to give than to receive because: (1) It makes us more like God, who gave his Son to die for us. (2) One who gives with the right motive, becomes more like Christ, who gave his life for us. (3) GOD REWARDS THE GIVER BUT DOES NOT REWARD THE RECEIVER. (4) The great apostle Paul set us an example, in meekness and humility. (5) The Early Christians gave not only their property but their lives for the cause of Christ. (6) God is glorified in our giving. (Matthew 5:16; 2 Corinthians 9:12, 13.)

Fifty two years ago, in Charleston, Mississippi, I met a dear, Christian woman, whose philosophy of life was based on giving instead of getting. She never gave Christmas presents, but made it her aim to plan, purpose and have ready a gift for someone EVERY DAY IN THE YEAR. Sometimes she could say like Peter, "Silver and gold have I none; but what I have, that give I thee." (Acts 3:6.) She gave freely of her time, love and service, in various ways. For instance she gave herself by a visit to a sick person or one shut-in; a cheerful word to the downhearted; comfort to the bereaved and to others in distress. Often she would sew for widows and orphans who needed clothing. One Thanksgiving she cooked a delicious dinner of turkey, dressing, cranberry sauce, vegetables and a dessert and took it to the Alms House, where they were dining on beans and bread, their regular fare. She and her husband ate a cold sandwich at home, and were happy because they had something to share. (Luke 14:12–14.)

"Because I have been given much, I, too, shall give;
Because of Thy great bounty, Lord, Each day I live.
I shall divide my gifts from Thee
With every brother that I see,
Who has the need of help from me."

— *Grace N. Crowell*

Christ, The World's Greatest Gift

Girls especially at this time of the year are interested in gifts. Big packages, medium packages and small packages, in colorful wrappings fill us with excitement and curiosity. We wonder and wait.

As we wait for the great moment to come when we open packages, let us think about the world's greatest gift. "For God so loved the world, that he gave his only begotten Son, that whosoever believeth on him should not perish, but have eternal life." (John 3:16.) God loved and gave, Christ also loved and gave. (Phil. 2:5–8; John 10:17, 18.) God's gift, eternal life is the greatest gift that anyone can receive. Christ made the supreme sacrifice — gave his life — that we might live. Unselfish love manifests itself in giving. ONE MAY GIVE WITHOUT LOVING, BUT ONE CAN NOT LOVE WITHOUT GIVING.

Our gifts to God are manifestations of our faith and love. Little faith and little love − little gifts. Great faith and great love − great gifts. "Even so faith, if it have not works, is dead in itself." (James 2:17.) One might ask: "How much of my time, energy and money shall I give to the Lord?" The answer is: "HOW MUCH FAITH AND LOVE DO YOU HAVE FOR YOUR LORD?"

God nowhere in the New Testament stipulated the amount for his children to give. Therefore we are guided by principles of giving.

1. The Macedonians gave themselves first, then out of deep poverty they gave liberally, beyond their power. (1 Corinthians 8:5.)

2. Give regularly, on the first day of the week, as we prosper. (1 Corinthians 16:2.)

3. Give cheerfully, as we purpose, not grudgingly or of necessity. (2 Corinthians 9:7.)

4. Readiness must be there. (2 Corinthians 8:12.)

5. If we sow sparingly, we shall reap sparingly. (2 Corinthians 9:6.)

"Give and it shall be given unto you . . . " (Luke 6:38.)

If anyone ever asks: "How much money do I have to give to the Lord?" The answer is: "Not one cent do you have to give, it must be a free will gift." It is true that when love enters the heart, "have to" passes out. When "have to" enters the heart, love passes out.

As an example of this principle let us suppose that a person has a mother that is old, feeble and sick. Would she ask her friends: "How much do you think I should do for my mother? I am willing to do as much as my brothers and sisters will do." Perhaps she should ask herself: "What did my mother do for me? She entered the valley of the shadow of death to bring me into the world. She gave me tender, loving care when I was a helpless infant." That is very true and we know that it is an ungrateful child who is not willing to supply the necessities of life for mother.

There is a responsibility that children have toward their parents. However, there is another obligation of importance. Jesus did something for me that my mother could not do. He died on the cross to save my soul.

Should one ever ask: "What do I have to do for my Lord and his church?" Please remember the words of the Lord Jesus that he himself said, "It is more blessed to give than to receive." (Acts 20:35.)

As the New Year approaches, my wish for all the readers of this column is: "Beloved, I pray that in all things thou mayest prosper and be in health, even as thy soul prospereth." (3 John 2.) One way that we all can prosper in a material way as well as spiritually is by giving generously to the cause of Christ. Girls, as Christians, make a resolution to begin the New Year by giving a portion of your allowance or earnings to God and you will be greatly blessed.

Success And Character Traits

Thomas Alva Edison lived to a ripe old age, but his mental grasp did not appear to be diminished as a result of his years.

Shortly before his death, he announced his formula for success, which was three ingredients: (1) ambition; (2) imagination; (3) the will to work.

Someone has introduced us to the Success Family, as follows: The father of Success is WORK, the mother of Success is AMBITION. The oldest son is COMMON SENSE, and some of the other boys are, STABILITY, ENTHUSIASM and COOPERATION. The oldest daughter is CHARACTER and her sisters are, CHEERFULNESS, LOYALTY, COURTESY, CARE, ECONOMY, SINCERITY and HARMONY. The baby is OPPORTUNITY. Get acquainted with the "old man" and you will be able to get along pretty well with the whole family.

THE WINDS OF FATE

One ship drives east and another drives west
With the selfsame winds that blow.
'Tis the set of the sails
And not the gales
Which tells us the way we go.

Like the winds of the sea are the ways of fate,
As we voyage along through life:
'Tis the set of a soul
That decides its goal,
And not the calm or the strife.

— *Ella Wheeler Wilcox*

Cheerfulness

We read in Proverbs 17:22 that "A cheerful heart is a good medicine." At times we all need medicine, and when that time comes we want it to be good. We all know that a trip to the drug store with a doctor's prescription can cost us money. Perhaps we think that it is cheaper to be cheerful than to get sick, which is really true. The mind affects the health to a remarkable degree. We are told that every third bed in the hospital is filled by a patient whose illness is not altogether physical, but caused by some kind of mental anxiety. Our family doctor, in Tenneessee, many years ago, said: "The three F's (fear, famine and fatigue) cause more sickness than disease germs."

The wise old doctor not only dispensed pills, but also good cheer. He encouraged his patients to rid themselves of worry, eat properly and get enough rest.

Most of us are guilty of worry, dread and anxiety. Famine of course is starving to death, not deliberately, but by improper diet. Fatigue is bodily exhaustion caused by not getting enough rest. Work is good and exercise is necessary, but so is rest.

Teen-agers, more than any other age group are subject to the dangers of the three F's. Mothers of young children see that they eat, play and sleep properly, Senior citizens have learned by experience what is good for them (that is why they are still living) so they regulate their habits accordingly: discard stressful emotions, eat a simple diet regularly, also work and rest in right amounts. The middle age group is composed of persons so busily engaged in making a living, and raising their families that they avoid the dangers of the three F's.

The teens are prone to worry about being popular and

keeping in step with the gang. They are anxious to be grown-up and shake off all parental control and "Do their own thing" and "Live their own life." They have very intense feelings of love and hate, likes and dislikes. Duriing these years they must get adjusted to the work-a-day world in job training, as well as the pressure of school work.

How many teenagers eat right? Diet is a big factor in staying well. To over-eat is bad. Between meal snacking on junk food is common practice. Likewise, the other extreme of a strict diet, without getting the proper nourishment is not good.

Because normally, the young are so full of energy and vitality that they never know when to stop and rest, from either play or work. Our bodies are wonderful machines, but they will wear out faster if we do not take proper care of them. Read 1 Corinthians 3:16, 17 and 1 Corinthians 6:19, 20 very carefully. We are responsible for the treatment we give these valuable bodies, not only in avoiding the evils of alcohol, tobacco and drugs, but in taking adequate rest, to stay mentally alert and physically strong.

For the new year, let's resolve to be happy and healthy. Let's cultivate a cheerful spirit and spread cheer instead of gloom among our friends.

The pensive friends will quote words of wisdom to us; the sturdy friends will slap us on the back and vow to stand by us through thick and thin; the kind and sympathetic friends will let the tears run down their cheeks and hold our hands compassionately. All these things are good in their way, but the cheery souls who make us see the silver lining in the blackest clouds are the people who help us along life's road. They talk of sunshine and gladness; they turn our self-pity into self-forgetfulness, then our feeble stumblings along the humdrum road will become a triumphant march.

The cheerful friend does not always point out the bright side, but lives on the bright side — that makes all the difference! Let's resolve to be a cheerful friend!

BIBLE HEARTS

BROKEN HEART — "Jehovah is nigh unto them that are of a broken heart; and saveth such as are of a contrite spirit." (Psalm 34:18.)

CLEAN HEART — "Create in me a clean heart, O God; and renew a right spirit within me." (Psalm 51:10.)

WISE HEART — "The wise in heart shall be called prudent." (Proverbs 16:21.)

FOOLISH HEART — "The lips of the wise disperse knowledge; but the heart of the foolish doeth not so." (Proverbs 15:7.)

GLAD HEART — "A glad heart maketh a cheerful countenance; but by sorrow of the heart the spirit is broken." (Proverbs 15:13.)

PERFECT HEART — "Let your heart therefore be perfect with Jehovah our God, to walk in his statutes, and to keep his commandments, as at this day." (1 Kings 8:61.)

PROUD HEART — "Every one that is proud in heart is an abomination to Jehovah." (Proverbs 16:15.)

CHEERFUL HEART — "A cheerful heart is a good medicine." (Proverbs 17:22.)

SICK HEART — "Hope deferred maketh the heart sick." (Proverbs 13:12.)

PURE HEART — "Blessed are the pure in heart: for they shall see God." (Matthew 5:8.)

TENDER HEART — "Be ye kind one to another, tender-hearted, forgiving each other, even as God also in Christ forgave you." (Ephesians 4:32.)

Topics For Discussion:

1. Formal dinner party planned by Mary and Alice: guest list; entertainment.
2. Contrast banquet tables and couches, in the time of Jesus, with banquet tables of our times.
3. True meaning of Luke 14:12—14.
4. Carefully examine ourselves: are we selfish and clannish? Whom do we inivte for dinner?
5. Sum up Paul's speech to the elders of the church at Ephesus.
6. Six reasons why it should make us happier to give than to receive.
7. Example of Christian woman who gave a gift every day in the year.
8. One may give without loving but one can not love without giving.
9. Five principles of giving in the New Testament.
10. Our gifts to God are manifestations of our faith and love.
11. Edison's formula for success.
12. The Success Family.
13. The Winds of Fate.
14. "A cheerful heart is a good medicine."
15. Teens subject to the dangers of the three F's.
16. How to be a cheerful friend.